W9-AUE-283

Summary of Contents

THE PRINCIPLES OF SUCCESSFUL FREELANCING

BY **MILES BURKE**

The Principles of Successful Freelancing

by Miles Burke

Copyright © 2008 SitePoint Pty. Ltd.

Expert Reviewer: Myles Eftos
Managing Editor: Chris Wyness
Technical Editor: Toby Somerville
Technical Editor: Andrew Tetlaw
Technical Director: Kevin Yank
Printing History:

   First Edition: December 2008

Editor: Hilary Reynolds
Index Editor: Fred Brown
Cover Design: Alex Walker

Published by SitePoint Pty. Ltd.

48 Cambridge Street
Collingwood VIC Australia 3066
Web: www.sitepoint.com
Email: business@sitepoint.com

ISBN 978-0-9804552-4-3
Printed and bound in Canada

About the Author

Miles Burke has been creating web sites since 1994. In 2002, Miles founded Bam Creative, an award-winning Western Australian web company. Miles serves as Chairperson of the Australian Web Industry Association, and has been awarded for his entrepreneurship in recent years; he's a recipient of the Contribution to the Web Industry award in 2005, winner of the WA Business News' 40under40 award in 2007, and appears in the 2008 edition of *Who's Who in Western Australia*. Miles can also be found writing at Miles' Blog: http://www.milesburke.com.au/blog/.

About the Expert Reviewer

Myles Eftos is a Perth-based web developer who jumped on the Rails express and never looked back. He is the event coordinator for the Australian Web Industry Association, which explains why most of their events are at the pub near his house.

About the Technical Editors

Toby Somerville is a serial webologist, who caught the programming bug back in 2000. For his sins, he has been a pilot, a blacksmith, a web applications architect, and a freelance web developer. In his spare time, he likes to kite buggy and climb stuff.

Andrew Tetlaw has been tinkering with web sites as a web developer since 1997. Before that, he worked as a high school English teacher, an English teacher in Japan, a window cleaner, a car washer, a kitchen hand, and a furniture salesman. He is dedicated to making the world a better place through the technical editing of SitePoint books and kits. He is also a busy father of five, enjoys coffee, and often neglects his blog at http://tetlaw.id.au/.

About the Technical Director

As Technical Director for SitePoint, Kevin Yank keeps abreast of all that is new and exciting in web technology. Best known for his book *Build Your Own Database Driven Website Using PHP & MySQL*, now in its third edition, Kevin also writes the *SitePointTech Times*, a free weekly email newsletter that goes out to over 150,000 subscribers worldwide.

When he isn't speaking at a conference or visiting friends and family in Canada, Kevin lives in Melbourne, Australia; he enjoys flying light aircraft and performing improvised comedy theater with Impro Melbourne. His personal blog, *Yes, I'm Canadian*, can be found at http://yesimcanadian.com/.

About SitePoint

SitePoint specializes in publishing fun, practical, and easy-to-understand content for web professionals. Visit http://www.sitepoint.com/ to access our books, newsletters, articles, and community forums.

To my wife and soul mate, Meredith.

To my children—Davis, Leia, and our latest addition, Quinn, who arrived during the writing of this book.

Table of Contents

Chapter 5   Win the Work

Preface

When I started designing web sites as a freelancer in 1994, I would have loved to have had the guidance of a book such as this one. The number of mistakes I made back then meant that it wasn't long before I returned to work as an employee, and it took two more attempts at full-time freelancing before it really started to become viable in 2002. During my years as a web designer and developer, creative director, and new media director for other companies, I learned much of what appears within these covers. I believe the mistakes I've made were just as important a learning tool as the successes I've had.

Although I specifically discuss web designers and developers, many of the principles covered in this book could be applied across many positions, even other industries. If there's an underlying message you can take away from this book, I hope it is that you should never fear trying something and never stop yearning for more knowledge and experience.

If you have talent as a web professional, it's almost certain that with some effort and knowledge, you will be able to fulfil your dream of working for yourself. The mere fact that you've picked up this book means you've already got the drive—now, you'll learn enough to have a fantastic chance of freelancing success!

Who Should Read This Book?

This book is intended as a guide to approaching the decision to be your own boss, effecting a smooth transition into a freelance career, and making it a success once you're there. The book's holistic approach ensures that it not only covers how to make your freelancing journey a financial success, but also how to do it without risking your health and sanity.

If you're considering freelancing, and are currently employed or have recently graduated, but are worried about diving head-first into the unknown, this book is for you. And if you've recently made the leap into freelancing but are struggling, this book will show you the way.

What's in This Book?

Chapter 1: Considering Freelancing?

What's it like to be a freelancer? Is it a life of complete control, working when you want, picking and choosing only the projects that interest you? Or is it a life of stress, working all hours, and wondering when your invoices will be paid so that you can afford your next meal? This chapter will show you the reality of freelancing, its advantages and disadvantages, and help you decide whether the freelancing life is for you.

Chapter 2: Prepare for the Transition

Having decided to take the plunge, this chapter will guide you through the planning process essential to a successful transition into the freelancing lifestyle. You'll perform a SWOT analysis, create a business plan that sets out your goals and milestones, begin thinking about your business's brand, and establish relationships with associates and contacts you may need to rely upon.

Chapter 3: Manage Your Money

How much should you charge per hour? How do you calculate your operating costs? How do you deal with debtors? Should you hire an accountant? Chapter 3 is all about money—and how, with a little forethought, it should never become a nightmare.

Chapter 4: Set Yourself Up

Now that your finances are under control, it's time to get productive. Chapter 4 leads you through everything you need to consider in order to stay productive, happy, and healthy. We discuss planning your office, ergonomics, time tracking, organizing your tools, and how you can separate your work from the rest of your life.

Chapter 5: Win the Work

Now it's time to make use of your new-found productivity and start bringing in the work! This chapter is all about creating your brand, developing your unique selling position, understanding the sales process, and overcoming your fear of selling.

Chapter 6: Give Great Service

Chapter 6 explains the basics and the benefits of giving great customer service. It's crucial to consider this component of your freelancing duties, even when you're up to your neck in project work. This chapter also deals with project management, clear communication, and the thorny subject of resolving issues with difficult clients.

Chapter 7: Achieve Work–Life Balance

As a freelancer it's often easy to forget about your work–life balance, emotional and physical health, and support of your community and the environment. Chapter 7 is all about ensuring your long-term well-being and engaging with the world beyond your office walls.

Chapter 8: Where to from Here?

Congratulations! You've built a successful freelancing business. Naturally, you'll now start to ask yourself where to go from here. You've reached decision time. What's the next step, the further challenge? You could stay freelancing as a single entity into the future, you may decide to hang up your tool belt and leave the freelance life, or you may decide to take the leap and grow your business beyond yourself.

The Book's Web Site

Located at http://www.sitepoint.com/books/freelancer1/, the web site that supports this book will give you access to the following facilities:

Updates and Errata

No book is perfect, and we expect that watchful readers will be able to spot at least one or two mistakes before the end of this one. The Errata page on the book's web site (http://www.sitepoint.com/books/freelancer1/errata.php) will always have the latest information about known errors.

The SitePoint Forums

If you'd like to communicate with us or anyone else on the SitePoint publishing team about this book, you should join SitePoint's online community.[1]

In fact, you should join that community even if you don't want to talk to us, because a lot of fun and experienced web designers and developers hang out there. It's a good way to learn new stuff, get questions answered in a hurry, and just have fun.

The SitePoint Newsletters

In addition to books like this one, SitePoint publishes free email newsletters, including *The SitePoint Tribune* and *The SitePoint Tech Times*. Reading them will keep you up to date on the latest news, product releases, trends, tips, and techniques for all aspects of web development. Sign up to one or more SitePoint newsletters at http://www.sitepoint.com/newsletter/.

Your Feedback

If you can't find an answer through the forums, or if you wish to contact us for any other reason, the best place to write to is books@sitepoint.com. We have a well-staffed email support system set up to track your inquiries, and if our support team members are unable to answer your question, they'll send it straight to us. Suggestions for improvements, as well as notices of any mistakes you may find, are especially welcome.

Conventions Used in This Book

You'll notice that we've used certain typographic and layout styles throughout this book to signify different types of information. Look out for the following items:

---

[1] http://www.sitepoint.com/forums/

Tips, Notes, and Warnings

Hey, You!

Tips will give you helpful little pointers.

Ahem, Excuse Me ...

Notes are useful asides that are related—but not critical—to the topic at hand. Think of them as extra tidbits of information.

Make Sure You Always ...

... pay attention to these important points.

Watch Out!

Warnings will highlight any gotchas that are likely to trip you up along the way.

Acknowledgments

I'd like to start by thanking you, the reader. Without you buying books and expanding your knowledge, there would be no opportunity for authors to share their thoughts in the printed form. Long live the Internet *and* the book.

Producing a book is indeed a group effort. I'd like to thank the publishing team at SitePoint for giving me this fantastic opportunity; particularly Simon Mackie and Chris Wyness, Managing Editors, who expertly steered this project. Thanks to Toby Somerville and Andrew Tetlaw, the Technical Editors, and Hilary Reynolds, language editor, who caressed my words into something far more eloquent. Thanks also to Myles Eftos, Expert Reviewer, who provided me with much-needed input.

All of the illustrations throughout this book are the work of Jay Hollywood, one of the team at Bam Creative and a gifted designer who interpreted my vague briefs into the great figures contained herein. Thanks, Jay!

Thanks to all my colleagues, clients, suppliers, and staff, both current and previous, who have helped me shape my ideas and given me the knowledge that I share here.

A warm thanks to Derek Featherstone, Mark Boulton, Molly E. Holzschlag, and Stephen Collins, who all granted me an interview. This book is far more valuable with your input. Thank you all for your patience, insight, and friendship.

Thanks to my parents for teaching me the value of good ethics and hard work. I wouldn't be writing this book without these important lessons.

My wife and children make me complete. I can never thank my wife, Meredith, enough for the patience she has shown me over the last few months as I snuck away in the evenings to write. All while you were either pregnant or handling life with a newborn child. This book is a testament to the fact that you allow me to undertake these projects without complaint or criticism. Thanks also to Davis, Leia, and Quinn, for being wonderful little people. I look forward to reading this book to all of you for bedtime stories, and I know you will have your own valuable advice to share.

1

Considering Freelancing?

You've probably heard your freelancer acquaintances boasting about lives of luxury, plenty of time off, the freedom to work when inspiration strikes and not before, no control-freak bosses, and dream projects of their choosing. Then again, other freelancers may have told you about working all night to meet deadlines, stressing between projects, missing regular social contact, and chasing clients who resist paying their bills.

The experience of freelancing, for most people, lies somewhere between these scenarios. You'll enjoy the chance to chill out in front of the TV during the day if you feel the need, yet you may have the occasional scare when you realize you don't know how you'll afford to eat next week. You will love the excitement of creating your own destiny; at the same time, there'll be moments when you wish someone else could make the right decisions for you!

So, before you decide to trade in your day job, you need to be aware of the advantages and disadvantages of the solo worker life, as well as understand the all-important range of skills and attributes of the successful freelancer.

Let's start by discussing the nature of freelancing, why you should consider such an option, its advantages and disadvantages, and the four main skills you need to become a successful freelancer.

Then, we'll look at some specific personality traits of successful freelancers, do some research, consider your particular situation, and end this chapter by making the acquaintance of some fledgling freelancers by way of a case study.

What Is Freelancing?

The term **freelancer** was first seen in Sir Walter Scott's *Ivanhoe* in the late 1700s, from the words "free" and "lance." Scott used it to refer to a medieval mercenary—a sort of roving soldier in the middle ages, who didn't particularly care for morals, ethics, or even whom he fought. It's probably not the ideal approach to a career nowadays, and this book hasn't been written for those types, although it's possible we'd all appreciate having some skills in jousting and swordplay up our sleeves when those projects go wrong.

Nowadays, a freelancer is defined as someone who sells his or her services to employers or clients without a long-term contract.

Freelancers often deal directly with their clients, or possibly work as a contractor to a number of larger businesses, which then on-sell the freelancer's services to their own client base. In the main, working as a freelancer implies that you don't have staff working for you, and that you frequently work for more than one client.

It's fair to say that nowadays there are more freelancers working in diverse fields than ever before, and much of this explosion is directly related to the rise of the Web. The Internet has been responsible for a huge jump in the numbers of freelancers operating around the globe. The ease of electronic communication, ability to develop virtual teams among other freelancers online, and broad acceptance of freelancing has meant that over the past decade or so it has become a highly popular career choice for millions of people.

The most common industries in which freelancers dwell in abundance, apart from the Web, are knowledge-based professions such as copywriting, photography, business consulting, information technology, journalism, marketing, and graphic design. Many of these offline professionals have a role in our online sphere as suppliers or consultants, and many of the principles discussed in this book would apply to their world as well.

However, this book will discuss principles of successful freelancing as the relate specifically to the Web; if you are a web designer or web developer considering going it alone, this is for you.

Why Freelance?

There are many pros and cons when it comes to freelancing, as we'll see, and a whole range of factors about your current situation need to be seriously considered before you hand your boss the letter of resignation.

First of all, freelancing is not for everyone. Although many people find that the advantages outweigh the potential pitfalls, sooner or later some people will decide that they're just not comfortable with the freelance life.

Advantages of the Freelance Life

flexible working hours

The ability to work the hours you want is a huge advantage for most people. Family commitments and school runs, part-time study, or simply your internal body clock's unique cycle may mean that you prefer to work early in the morning, or late into the evening.

 Watching Weird Work Hours

Having flexible hours does not mean that most of your clients are likely to feel as strongly as you that 2.00 a.m. is the best time to be working. You'll likely find that after enough 9.00 a.m. phone calls and meetings, it's best to fall in line with business hours for at least part of your day.

flexible work location

When you first consider freelancing, you'll probably glance around your own home, determining where you'll create your office space and deciding that you can finally justify that shiny red espresso machine. Certainly, it is highly desirable to have some space at home that's quiet, comfortable, interruption-free, and conducive to work.

However, don't discount the concept of being truly mobile—many cafes and libraries now have free wireless Internet, or you can arrange your own mobile wireless broadband. You can also treat these locations as a complement to your home office; this can help to counter the monotony of working in isolation. You'll likely meet other local freelancers doing the same as you!

choice of projects

We've all had the experience of working on a project or for a client that promised to turn into a nightmare from the outset, which we'd prefer to have avoided if we'd had a say in the matter. As a freelancer, once you're established, you're in control—you have the opportunity to refuse projects or clients.

being in charge

The feeling of strength and autonomy that comes from being in charge of your life's direction is a major drawcard. For many people, this is the main reason to head down the freelancing path.

constant education

It's no coincidence that many people attracted to the freelance lifestyle also have an unquenchable thirst for knowledge. Freelancing can allow you the flexibility to spend more time on research and planned education than would a normal nine-to-five job. Want to read that new typography book, or catch up on that agile development blog? Sure, jump right on in; no one's looking over your shoulder, and the time is yours to spend as you please—deadlines permitting.

wide variety of projects

Unlike an in-house salaried position—where you may find yourself slaving away on the same mind-numbing web application or site for twelve months because you're assigned to do so—you have the opportunity to work across multiple industries and switch your focus between large and small projects.

freedom in clothing choice

Last but not least, a number of people have reported to me that the prospect of being able to wear what they wanted was a definite factor in their decision to go freelance. Being able to shed the suit, tie, make-up, and high heels—whichever apply!—in favor of shorts and a T-shirt has a certain appeal for many.

Don't throw that suit out, though; you may still need it upon occasion for client meetings!

Disadvantages of the Freelance Life

financial insecurity

Easily the biggest disadvantage for many people is that ocean effect upon the bank balance. Money tends to come in and go out with an ebb-and-flow cycle, especially when you've just started out. One week you'll feel rich, revelling in your self-made status; the next you'll be wondering how you'll put gas in the car.

This problem can largely be avoided by understanding, controlling, and being acutely aware of your cash flow. However, for many people the unpredictability of finances becomes the reason they return to full-time employment after a period of freelancing. We'll cover strategies to avoid these issues in Chapter 3.

loneliness

It's not uncommon for freelancers to feel absolutely cut off from the rest of the world, especially if they're single and working from home. This can be alleviated by joining local freelance or micro business networks, and making the effort to socialize after work hours with friends and family. If you're busy, it can be all too easy to feel that you can't justify spending time on such frivolity.

blurring of home and work times

Flexible work hours can be a double-edged sword. Without a high level of self-control and a strict understanding of when you're working and when you're at leisure, you risk burning yourself out by working around the clock.

This can, of course, also become an issue when your clients start thinking they can call you anytime. It mightn't seem like a problem at first, but those early Sunday morning calls will soon make you feel otherwise.

wearing all those different hats

Not only do you find that you don't have as much free time as you'd hoped, but those tasks that absorb a lot of your time you probably don't even want to *know* about: selling, marketing, bookkeeping, dealing with legal matters, debt collecting, and the like.

loss of salaried benefits

These benefits are often overlooked. Freelancers are susceptible to letting themselves down when it comes to health benefits, holiday planning, superannuation, and insurance. Other "soft benefits" you may have taken for granted, such as the gym membership, a vehicle allowance, or even use of the company car, can be sorely missed when they're not there anymore.

With the tightened purse-strings of the starting phase of your freelance life, it's tempting to put these essentials aside—and risk being caught short when you unexpectedly need them.

Are You Freelance Material?

One of the hardest yet most rewarding personal development steps you can ever take is to discover what you are good at, and where you have areas that can use development. Accepting our own limitations can help make all of us better people.

When it comes to web design and development, it's a demanding industry—even more so if you're freelancing. However, although the freelance life may seem hard at times, successful freelancers never look back.

Successful freelancers often start by evaluating their own skills and personality, especially their ability to work solo. Once you have a clear understanding of your areas of weakness and what you need to improve upon, you have solid goals to work toward.

Although you may feel that you have all the technical competencies to manage the freelance role, you'll soon find that there is far more to being successful as a freelancer than the ability to write great code or design the coolest layouts.

The skills required for being a great freelancer can be broken down to four distinct areas, as shown in Figure 1.1: technical, business, organizational, and interpersonal.

Figure 1.1. The four skills areas of the successful freelancer

Technical Skills

For a developer, possessing technical skills means that you're technically competent in your language or languages of choice: PHP, Ruby on Rails, Microsoft .NET, and the like. As a designer, you'd consider the strength of your skills in design software, color theory, typography, and overall design knowledge.

As a designer or developer, you need to feel confident in your own technical ability, as this is what you're going to be relying upon. You can't just lean over to a coworker's desk and ask about anything you're not sure of! Consider your areas of weakness, and research what's involved in strengthening these areas—you'll probably find that they're easier to fill out than you thought.

Business Skills

It's vitally important to have, or at least be aware of, the fundamentals of business before you consider running your own. If you plan to succeed, you'll need a solid understanding of cash flow, marketing, time management, customer service, and other areas. Many of these elements can be outsourced, as we'll see in Chapter 2, but you'll still need a working knowledge of all of them.

Organizational Skills

Your ability to be well organized, or at the very least to keep on top of those dreary administrative duties, will be paramount to your success. Start by reading personal productivity books and blogs, and research the different techniques of organization.

Don't go overboard though; you could end up being hampered by trying too many productivity methods and not doing enough actual work! You'll soon find a method you feel happy with, which can be defined in this context as feeling that you have the smooth running of your business under control.

Interpersonal Skills

You may think that the freelance life would suit the shy or socially inept recluse, beavering away alone. Unfortunately, however, an aversion to social contact could limit your opportunities more than you think.

Productive interaction with clients and prospective clients, not to mention your suppliers, will become a crucial part of your success, so embrace human contact and be personable.

Successful Freelancer Personality Traits

As you meet freelancers of all varieties, you'll be struck by how different they are. The very nature of the freelance lifestyle suggests that it attracts individuals, independent thinkers, creative personalities—all sorts of people who have, for their own reasons, decided that the nine-to-five working-for-somebody-else full-time employment model is not for them.

Typically, though, these are the predominant personality traits and abilities you'll be likely to find in a successful freelancer:

- ambition
- an aptitude for problem solving
- courage
- a mature outlook
- a high level of communication skills
- a strong work ethic
- perfectionism
- a professional attitude
- self-confidence

When weighing up your own compatibility with such a work choice, it's important to consider these traits. You'll ideally possess more than a few of these qualities, if not all of them.

In real-life terms, this means that to be a successful freelancer, you should be able to find resonance in many of the following characteristics; ideally, you:

- believe organization includes keeping the workspace tidy and planning ahead
- form short-term and long-term plans, preferably detailed on paper
- remain calm and able to work through issues in times of stress
- are able to handle a high level of responsibility
- understand that research goes beyond a two-minute Google search
- appreciate the role of financial planning
- are passionate about design or development, or both
- understand that budgeting means planning ahead, not spending every cent as it comes in
- value your health as important, so that you exercise and get regular checkups
- consider freelancing because you believe you can be successful, not just to escape your current job
- understand selling and embrace the process
- have a good support network of family and friends

- acknowledge that cash flow is vital to success
- appreciate that education is a continual process, not a once-off effort to gain a qualification
- plan towards gaining a work–life balance, and not work round the clock
- realize that customer service is about empathy and understanding, not just saying sorry after the fact

When looking at the four areas of skills and the personality traits above, you may begin to feel a twinge of self-doubt. That's absolutely normal and healthy. If you weren't at all nervous about taking the plunge, you'd be crazy!

And of course, if you don't tick all of the boxes, it doesn't mean you won't be a great freelancer. Nor will it guarantee your immediate freelance success to claim that each point fits you like a glove. However, if these points do ring a bell with you to some degree, you'll be in excellent shape to work your way to a great freelance career.

To reiterate: a successful freelancer is one who plans, who understands that the role is varied, who acknowledges his or her limitations, and who realizes there's far more to the role than writing code or creating designs. If these desirable attributes haven't scared you off completely, you're probably an ideal candidate for the free-lance life.

Making the Decision

There's much to be considered before you enter the unknown world of freelancing. You'll need to weigh up the cost of security against that of freedom, and your own situation will determine which way you jump, or even how *far* you jump. Reading this book will give you insight into how to avoid putting all your eggs in one basket straight away.

And remember: at the end of the day, it's fine to accept that you've tried freelancing, but want to return to full-time work.

Do Your Research

In terms of research, you are already taking the right step in reading this book. However, it's important to seek as many opinions and tips as possible to help you make this potentially life-changing decision. You'll find many blogs authored by freelancers on the Web, as well as discussion forums and networking groups frequented by other freelancers.

Examples include a popular blog for freelance web professionals called Freelance Folder,[1] the freelance discussion forums site TalkFreelance,[2] and the aptly named Wake Up Later.[3]

Ask around at your local web industry groups, and keep a finger on the pulse for freelance or entrepreneur events in your city. Speak with as many people who have gone before you as you possibly can. It's amazing how open most seasoned freelancers are about their experiences, and how helpful seeking their advice can be!

Consider Your Situation

If you've reached this point of the chapter, weighed yourself against the summary of desirable attributes we saw earlier, and are still determined to try your hand at going it alone, great! It's highly likely that you will be very successful at freelancing.

Now, before you do anything else, take stock of your current situation. There are some other important considerations here beyond your own personality and skills.

Firstly, do you have any savings? If not, start saving right away—having a small cushion, should there be some tight months when you're starting out, is essential and something I cannot overstate. Having the buffer of that piggybank, even if you never need to break into it, is well worth the effort and time it takes to gather it before you leap into the unknown (we'll see more of this subject in Chapter 3). So how much do you need to save? This is something only you can determine, and depends on your situation. If you live at home with your parents, or share the rent with flatmates, and have little or no debt, you can probably survive on less income for a longer period than someone who has a mortgage and children to feed. Ideally, you would have three months of costs up your sleeve. Consider your expectations of lifestyle, weigh up what you need in order to live, and think about what you can bear to give up so that you can start to fill that piggybank.

---

[1] http://freelancefolder.com/
[2] http://www.talkfreelance.com/
[3] http://www.wakeuplater.com/

Secondly, do you have adequate room available at home for an office? You need to set up somewhere quiet, with little scope for interruption, and preferably access to natural light, as well as able to accommodate a desk, chair, shelving, and everything else you'll need. You should plan to have a room devoted to your business—working out of a corner of your bedroom isn't ideal in the long term.

Thirdly, if you have a partner or family, what are their thoughts? If your partner isn't supportive of your decision to go freelance, it can cause great strain on the relationship and create stress that you'd be better off without. Take the time to explain your plans, and ensure that you share your accomplishments with your loved ones, every step of the way.

Lastly, do you already own the necessary hardware and software? Look beyond the standard code and design tools—will you need special accounting software, or additional tools such as a fax machine or filing cabinet? Start a list of the items you'll require as you work your way through this book; we'll deal with this in more detail when we get to Chapter 4.

Interview with Derek Featherstone

Based in Ottawa, Canada, Derek Featherstone is a well-known instructor, speaker, and web developer with expertise in accessibility consulting. He has eight years' experience of running his own web development and accessibility consultancy, Further Ahead.[4]

Derek advises many government agencies, educational institutions, and private sector companies, providing them with expert accessibility testing and review, and recommendations for improving the accessibility of their web sites to all people—his web site page (shown in Figure 1.2), with its list of speaking engagements, shows how busy he is! He's also a member of The Web Standards Project, and serves on two taskforces: Accessibility/Assistive Devices and DOM Scripting.

---

[4] http://www.furtherahead.com/

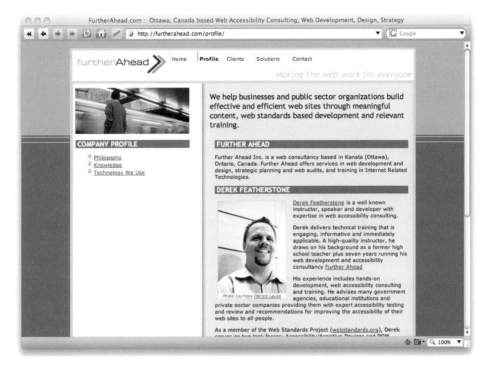

Figure 1.2. The web site of Further Ahead

I asked Derek a few questions about freelancing:

What made you take the leap into working for yourself?

I first saw the tremendous opportunities of freelancing when my wife left her job to go into business for herself. Any limitations on the success of her business were her own, not from external forces. She was the decision-maker, and she held her own success in the palm of her hand. I wanted a taste of that too.

At the time, I felt burned out, overworked, and underpaid. Add to that massive stress from a new house, our first child on the way, next to no sleep, and a death in the family—it all resulted in a life-changing experience. I woke up one morning with Bell's Palsy—the left side of my face was completely paralyzed. In short, I was forced to question everything over the next three months, when I couldn't close my eye, smile, drink, or eat properly.

I realized I needed to change. I followed my wife's lead and decided to get out there and do my own thing.

What did you see as the main advantage of going freelance?

Before I went freelance, I knew that I didn't really have the flexibility I wanted. It really bothered me that someone else was deciding what constituted professional development activities on my behalf. There were ideas and techniques that I want to explore, but felt I couldn't.

The most immediate impact on me when I decided to go out on my own was that feeling of empowerment—that I was the one who got to determine my path. That, in itself, was the biggest advantage for me—the feeling that I was in control of my future, that I was the decision-maker.

What do you believe was the biggest challenge or disadvantage you faced in going freelance?

In many ways, that flexibility was the biggest challenge as well. My days were very structured before I started my own business, and that sudden flexibility and lack of structure made managing my workload quite difficult.

Very closely tied to that is the stable income that full-time employment provided. Suddenly, that was gone, so I had to get used to the fact that the flexibility I wanted came at a price.

Case Study: Emily and Jacob

Throughout this book, we'll be keeping an eye on two people as they head down the freelance path. I give you … Emily and Jacob!

About Emily

Emily has been a web developer for a large media company for the last five years. Previously, she completed a Computer Science degree.

Although her employment is good, Emily is considering freelancing as a career move. She is confident that she has all the technical skills she requires to go freelance, is highly organized, and has a good understanding of project management. Her main concern is that her administration skills may not be strong enough.

Emily rents a flat on her own, and has saved enough money to live a fairly meager existence for the first six months, should she be without cash flow.

About Jacob

Jacob completed his Graphic Design degree nearly ten years ago, and is a self-taught web designer. Jacob works for an IT company, but feels that, as the only designer, he lacks stimulation and certainly receives no respect for his craft.

He has been considering freelancing for a while, and has managed to saved enough to live on for about six weeks as a safety net; he feels fairly secure, though, as he currently lives with his parents.

Jacob is a natural networker, and has made a large number of contacts among the web industry in his state. He believes that he can capitalize on those connections by starting out on his own.

Summary

In this chapter, we've considered the pros and cons of freelancing. Before taking the leap into freelancing, you need to be aware of the advantages and disadvantages of such a work choice, as well as understanding and acknowledging the all-important range of skills and attributes of the successful freelancer. Are you inspired and motivated to taking control of your future—for all the right reasons?

We've undertaken a self-assessment exercise. Do you believe you have the right technical, business, organizational, and interpersonal qualities to become a success at freelancing?

We've discussed the importance of research. Ask as many freelancers as you can what worked for them when they started out. You'll very likely be motivated by their feedback.

We've considered your situation. Do you have the ability to draw on cash, if you need to? Are you able to set up a home office comfortably at your premises? Are your loved ones supportive and understanding?

And finally, we've met Emily and Jacob—two hypothetical freelancers with stars in their eyes, whose fortunes we will follow as we progress through this book. So continue reading! In the next chapter, you'll gain important lessons on the practical aspect of beginning freelance work.

Prepare for the Transition

The most exciting and eagerly anticipated phase of freelancing happens *after* all the planning—and we haven't quite reached it yet! There's good reason for putting the brakes on until we know exactly where we're going—a freelancer who has built a solid foundation of planning has a far better chance of surviving than a freelancer who hasn't prepared for the plunge.

In this chapter, we'll walk through a couple of options for heading down the freelance road, we'll make a start on the planning by looking at some elementary tools, and we'll establish the all-important goals and milestones.

Then we'll consider your trading name, create your start-up shopping list, and contemplate your business structure. We'll wrap all this up by discussing how to choose suppliers and whether you should consider outsourcing any bookkeeping and additional legal work.

Deciding How Far to Jump

Now that you've made the decision to become a freelancer, we've reached the point of short-, medium-, and long-term preparation. If you're anything like me, you'll want to jump in running as fast as you can. However, it's been proven time and again that to ensure the best chance of success, you should expend plenty of effort in planning and preparation. This raises the question of which work mode to begin your freelance life with: full-time or part-time.

If you're a student nearing the end of your studies, you've got a distinct time to work towards. (That said, I recommend that unless you have run a business previously, don't go freelance straight after graduating—spend some time in employment in your chosen field first, to get those skills polished.) This also applies if your current work is coming to a close—you may be on a fixed-term contract, or the company you've been working for is winding up. However, for many people, the entry to freelancing is a case of juggling full-time employment with preparations to exit the rat race.

There are advantages and disadvantages to both situations, and you'll need to weigh these up carefully. Let's take a moment to look at some of them.

Freelancing on the Side

There's a lot to be said for freelancing "on the side," at least in the beginning:

- This is a great way to test the waters without making that big jump.

- You can spend as much after-hours time as you need on planning your business.

- You can save just-in-case money for as long as it takes for you to feel comfortable before venturing into the unknown.

- You're able to be choosier with the work you take on, as your salary is still coming in to help with costs.

- If you don't have any good recent work to show, part-time freelancing allows you to build a great portfolio before you move to full-time.

- The clients you groom now are likely to be with you once you make that leap, helping with immediate cash flow.

- It allows you to take your time to fit out the home office, without blowing your starting budget.

- Freelancing part-time after hours, as well as holding down a full-time position, gives you the authentic taste of a busy week as a freelancer. This can help you determine your ability to cope with that amount of work at any given time.

There are a few disadvantages to this practice, though:

- Depending on your employment contract, you may be restricted from doing work that directly competes with services offered by your employer. It's best to approach your boss to discuss this.

- Most clients will want to contact you during their workday hours, which tend to be when you're busy at your full-time gig.

- You lose out on the all-important downtime hours of evenings and weekends. If you attract lots of work, you may end up exhausting yourself trying to work two jobs.

- You'll be cautious of growing too fast, given you have restricted hours in which to work. It can become tricky trying to keep everyone happy, and you may have to turn down new work in order not to fail existing clients.

Freelancing Full-time

There are some compelling advantages to jumping in with both feet:

- You'll have the freedom to set up your freelance life, instead of juggling it with a full-time job.

- Full-time start-up mode means that you have plenty of time in which to network, make important contacts, and meet prospects.

- There are no issues with your employer being aggrieved about you working freelance on the side, and you'll have no hesitation in taking on as many new clients and projects as you can handle.

There are, however, some disadvantages to full-time freelancing straight away:

- Nothing feeds self-doubt more than work failing to come in during those first few weeks.

■ The cash drain while you rush around making contacts and courting business can really hurt your back pocket.

■ The all-important planning tends to be the first casualty when those projects come in—understandably, you'll be more interested in taking an opportunity to earn some much-needed money than mapping out your legal business structure.

Taking Time to Plan

"Failures don't plan to fail, they fail to plan," says best-selling author and business motivational speaker, Harvey MacKay.[1]

If you are planning to start freelancing part-time, you should have the time to put together all of the plans and start saving for the just-in-case rainy-day money. On the other hand, if you plan to move straight into full-time freelancing, remember that you'll have those looming deadlines as soon as you take on projects. Even so, it doesn't mean that you should ignore planning or preparation.

For most people, the concept of business planning is likely to provoke a jaw-dislocating yawn. However, it's much more productive to welcome this as an exciting time, where you start to understand where you really want to travel on this freelance path. The world really is your oyster—you've made the emotional commitment, perhaps you already have some prospective clients lined up, and you may have already done much of this planning work in the back of your mind. It's invaluable to take a little time to write these thoughts and plans down, for future reference and as a way to refine and catalogue your thoughts.

Many freelancers and small businesses fail in their first few years, and it's widely agreed by experts that the number-one reason for such failure is because those business had little or no form of planning. This planning document doesn't need to be a huge tome of numbers and words; it really is the summation of what you have been thinking, committed to paper.

This document is where you start to list known and unknown areas of your plans, so you can elaborate on them over time. A good business plan is an evolving one,

---

[1] http://www.harveymackay.com/

so don't consider it a chore to be completed in an hour and then stuck in a desk drawer and forgotten about.

There are a myriad of web sites dedicated to sharing templates and ideas about what they consider a great business plan. Perhaps the most important element of a business plan is that you remain actively involved with it. Review it frequently, adjusting and editing it where required—especially during those first few months.

Your plan could be just a few pages, or it could be dozens, but unless you have grand plans to circulate it for investors or financial institutions to read, avoid using buzzwords and reams of useless blue-sky figures. The plan is for your eyes only, so keep it succinct and to the point, and an honest appraisal of the "who, what, when, and how" of your plans.

There are many elaborate methods for writing a solid business plan, but let's start by creating a text document, and answering what questions we can from the list in Example 2.1. For those questions to which you don't know the answer yet, just write the question, reminding yourself to add that material as you go.

Remember, plans change, so at this stage your efforts are likely to be more crystal-ball gazing than actual fact. You'll expand on the plan, filling it out in more detail as you work your way through this book and progress over the first weeks and months of freelancing. And it's fine to add other notes besides the questions included here—even if they're rough dot points, the more notes the better!

Creating a SWOT

The planning term **SWOT** first appeared in the 1960s. A SWOT analysis is really just a simple strategic planning method that helps evaluate projects and businesses. It's based around a four-square grid, shown in Figure 2.1, which covers Strengths, Weaknesses, Opportunities, and Threats. I've used it a number of times to help me make decisions around new products or service offerings under consideration, and it works just as well for business models.

Example 2.1. Business Planning Questions

summary
- What is the initial concept?
- What is your current situation?
- What will your key success factors be?
- What are your longer-term vision and goals?

market analysis
- What does the current market look like?
- What is your target market?
- What are the characteristics of your perfect client?
- What do your target clients require?

competitive overview
- What does your industry look like?
- Are there many competitors?
- Who are your five closest competitors?
- What products or services do they offer?
- What opportunities do you have to be unique? (Can you fill a niche or be different from your competitors in some way?)
- What are the risks and threats?

sales and marketing
- How will you attract clients?
- How can potential clients find you?
- What marketing activities would you consider?

plan of action
- What do you need to do in order to kick things off?
- What should you do in the medium term?
- What are some longer-term plans?

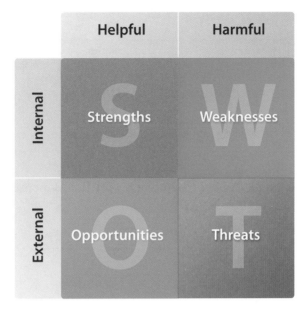

Figure 2.1. The SWOT grid explained

To start, list all of your strengths and weaknesses—these can be thought of as the internal elements, over which which you have some degree of control. Continue by identifying all of the opportunities and threats that you can—these are generally external forces, such as competitors and the industry at large. Then, look for ways to use your strengths, improve on your weaknesses, exploit the opportunities available to you, and fend off the threats.

A SWOT analysis certainly don't need to be as long-winded as it may sound; I have found some of the most useful SWOT analyses are those that fit onto a single page. By way of example, let's look at our very own Jacob and Emily.

Jacob has put together the beginnings of a SWOT, which looks like this:

Table 2.1. Jacob's SWOT Analysis

Strengths	Weaknesses	Opportunities	Threats
natural networker (great with people)	small savings, and has never run a business before	knows the industry, has a good understanding of market	many freelancers work nearby
fantastic portfolio of work	not proficient with code	has many contacts who may be prospects	larger firms offering a similar service

Emily, on the other hand, has put together a SWOT that is more like this:

Table 2.2. Emily's SWOT Analysis

Strengths	Weaknesses	Opportunities	Threats
has a wide range of skills	not very good at planning	only web developer freelancing in her local area	other people becoming freelancers
very hard working	perfectionist; sometimes takes more time to complete projects than she intends to	has a contract or two already lined up	lack of clients in small city

These examples are only a few lines long, but you can easily extend them to a page or more. The concept is really a succinct and useful method of establishing your pros and cons.

Establishing Goals and Milestones

All this talk of business-planning documents and SWOT analyses may be making your head spin, and you're forgiven if you find yourself glossing over them in your rush to make a tangible start on your own business. However, I strongly suggest that you take a moment to write down some simple goals and then define some milestones.

Goal-setting helps filter all of the thousands of thoughts and ideas you have into a list that's far more manageable. High achievers in every field from sports to business consistently suggest that goal-setting is an invaluable part of the process. Goals can help you define your objectives, help you to understand what's important to you, motivate you towards achievement, and build your self-confidence.

I find goal-setting is most helpful in distinguishing what's important and what's irrelevant. This helps me concentrate on what really is crucial to me, and gives me the freedom to spend less time on the rest.

Many people use the acronym **SMART** when creating goals, as well as for other project management methods. SMART stands for:

- **S**pecific: is the description of the goal precise?
- **M**easurable: do you explain how you will measure results?
- **A**ttainable: is it possible to achieve, with some effort?
- **R**ealistic: do you have the power to control the results?
- **T**imely: do you have a deadline for the goal?

The reasoning behind SMART holds that a vague goal is an almost useless goal. As an example, say I needed to win more projects; I could define a goal as, "Get more web site projects." Sure, this is better than nothing, but how much more inspiring would it be if I changed it to say, "Win five more web site projects this quarter."

See the difference? I've been specific (I want to win more projects); I've been measurable (I want five more in the next three months); my goal is attainable (who couldn't win five projects in three months?); my goal is realistic (I know I can deliver five projects within that time); and it's timely (it has a three-month deadline).

Setting a great goal should challenge and stimulate you. If I downsized my goal to winning one project in the next two months, I'd be more likely to slack off. It also needs to be realistic, though, so some impossible expectation of getting ten projects in three months would set up almost certain failure. It's a good idea to limit yourself to just a handful of short-term and medium-term goals—writing an exhaustive list of everything you would like to complete prior to your death is a sure way to demotivate yourself.

 Goal-setting Help

You may have heard of the popular Web 2.0 application, 43 Things.[2] This site presents a great example of goal-setting at work—try listing your goals on 43 Things, or simply use a text file or whiteboard, and see how you go!

---

[2] http://www.43things.com/

Now, when we think of milestones, we normally recall a large web project we've been involved in. Think of a milestone as a landmark towards your longer-term goals.

A typical milestone is to realize a situation where you're earning more than your current salary within a year of going solo. There are some smaller milestones you can place along the way to see how you're shaping up.

The first milestone would be having the ability to pay yourself enough to survive on. Let's say that's about half of what you earn today. Set a milestone based upon how long you believe it should take to reach this point—it may be a month, or perhaps three months, depending on your situation.

Now, let's consider your return on investment, which is initially to reclaim all of those start-up costs involved in your transition to freelance life. These vary, of course, from person to person, but you should have an idea of how long this would take.

The third milestone is that of bringing home the same salary as you currently earn. Will this take six months, or nine months, or even longer?

Write down your milestones and refer to them over the coming months—you'll be surprised how quickly you reach them, exceed them, and find yourself setting more goals for future success!

Planning the Start-up Shopping List

An important element of this big planning phase you'll need to do before (or while!) you're making your move to freelance is to start preparing yourself for some of the expenses you'll be faced with over the first few months.

Now, I'd like to say there won't be any costs, but that's simply not true. However, I *can* say that shopping around for the best deals, looking for opportunities to swap services with suppliers, and staggering your expenses will certainly alleviate the sting of spending money when all you want to do at this stage is earn a little.

There are immediate costs, depending on your current situation, and then there are costs that you can delay for a while. The best method of allowing for these costs is to create a list, prioritize what you need in which order (based on your current situation), and then expect the higher end of the price range. That way, when those costs work out to be cheaper than anticipated, it's a bonus for your bottom line.

"Must have" costs include:

- business card printing
- domain name registration
- web site hosting
- telephone costs
- hardware
- software licensing
- legal or licensing costs

"Should have" costs include:

- insurance for office contents
- income insurance or business continuity insurance (if you're able to be covered)
- office equipment (desk, chair, light, filing cabinets, printer, and so on)

Ideally, you would cover these costs at the same time as the must-haves, but the reality is most people won't be able to take such a budget hit in their first month of freelancing, so they can be slightly delayed.

 Thrifty Bargain Hunting!

Don't forget how much cheaper it is to seek out second-hand office furniture and equipment—you can find bargains through the likes of eBay, your local trading post, or used furniture stores. You can set yourself up with perfectly functional trappings at a fraction of the cost of all-new, shiny furniture.

"Nice to have" costs include items such as:

- new hardware
- dedicated servers
- magazine subscriptions
- industry association memberships

These would be great if you have the capital, but they can easily be delayed if circumstances dictate.

Through good planning and careful attention to your cash flow, these costs won't have as much impact as they may seem to have now. We'll go through finances in more detail in the next chapter.

 Leasing versus Buying

When it comes to any high-investment equipment you might need, leasing is a well-known method of improving your cash flow by paying a far smaller amount per month over the life of the lease.

Although the end result is that you pay more for the equipment than if you bought it outright, the benefits of having more cash on hand can be an excellent compromise. You'll often be surprised at the small difference in final figures, and realize the benefit of being able to hand the equipment back or upgrade it at the end of the lease term.

Creating Your Brand: the Preliminaries

We'll talk more about branding yourself in Chapter 5; however, it's very important that you carefully consider the business name you plan to use, when first kicking off your freelance career. There are two typical approaches: use your personal name, or create an entirely new trading name.

Let's look at these options in more detail.

Using Your Own Name

Using your own name is a fantastic way to build a personal brand. Taking this option depends on what your vision of the future looks like—if you plan to hire staff at a later date, you may want to avoid using your own full name, but there are still options available even if you do; for example, Burke Design & Development; Miles Burke & Co. On the other hand, if you have every intention of remaining a one-person show, giving yourself a name like "XYZ Corporation" can be considered misleading, as it won't take long for your clients to realize that you're a solo worker.

Anything's Possible!

Many people start off never expecting to take on staff. Don't rule this out, unless you feel strongly against it. I once couldn't picture myself hiring employees ... and at the time of writing I have 16!

This theory assumes your name is unique enough to be memorable, and that it's easy for your clients to pronounce. If your name is Bob Smith, you may find that it's too common for business registration and other registrations, such as domain names or intellectual property.

To recap, the advantages of using your personal name include:

- it builds a reputation around you
- it's normally easier to recall, since clients already know your name
- it can avoid misleading clients if you plan to stay solo
- it looks far more personal and (depending on the uniqueness of your name) can make you easier to find on the Web

Disadvantages of using your own name include:

- it limits you in terms of hiring staff and possibly even selling the business, if you reach that point someday
- it can make it harder to rank on search engines if your name is very common
- it may be hard to pronounce if your name is very uncommon

Using a Fictitious Name

Irrespective of the business structure, having a business name unrelated to your personal name has a number of considerations that need taking into account.

A business name which when read phonetically is still pronounced correctly is perfect. Pfizer could be a challenge; Sigma is fairly unambiguous. Don't get too clever with creating crazy business names—most people would regret having to answer the phone with the greeting "Smelly Shoe Design" before long.

Having your main service as part of the name makes sense as well, although be warned against making it *too* specific. For example, perhaps you're a designer whose short-term plans are to design web sites only. You'll need to consider whether you plan to expand into other forms of design in the future. Having a name like "XYZ Web Design" when you're pitching for a logo design project may not help you beat your competition, so beware of suggesting that you're only capable of providing one service.

A good name should be easy to recall, evocative, pronounceable, and unique. You'll want to register the domain name, so run a WHOIS on your shortlist to rule out those already registered. Don't just consider your own country extension—register as many extensions (including the top-level domains, .com and .net) as possible.

 Unexpected Domain Names

Take a step back and look at your domain name carefully! There's been more than one business that has come up with a great trade name and bought the (in)appropriate domain name to match:

- Experts Exchange: expertsexchange.com
- Therapist Finder: therapistfinder.com
- Powergen Italia: powergenitalia.com

The advantages of creating a new name for your business are:

- It keeps your personal and business lives further separated.
- It allows infinite choice of business name.
- It allows you to tailor the name according to domain name availability.
- It's easier to sell your business or client base in the future.

Disadvantages of using a custom name include:

- You'll need to exert some energy to get a new name to stick.
- You could have issues finding one that you feel comfortable with and fits you well.
- It's not an easy process to change the name later on.

If you do decide to use a created name, start by creating a shortlist of options, and then create a spreadsheet. Populate the first column by doing a WHOIS search and finding which domain names are still available (both geographic and top-level).

Table 2.3. Business domain name matrix

Name	.com	.net	.us
XYZ Design Factory	available	available	available
XYZ	taken	taken	available
XYZ Web Works	available	available	available

Then, fire up your favorite search engine and search for those business names. What are the results? You wouldn't be the first start-up to make it this far, only to find another product or business using the same name. It's better to do this research now, rather than when the business cards have been printed … Try predictable misspellings of the words, too—often a business name may be only one letter different from another, so make sure you check first!

Thirdly, consult your local trademark database and see if there are any trademarks of which you need to be aware. Even very similar words may be worth avoiding.

You should also speak to some friends and colleagues. Ask them what they think of each name in your refined shortlist, and narrow this list down even further. It's better to do this face to face to observe an immediate reaction, rather than by email or phone, where they may have a longer time to consider it—you want their gut response.

Finally, go with your instinct. After all, it's your creation, and you have to like it. If, after hours and hours of soul-searching, you just aren't happy with your choice, try again or consider using your own name.

Example 2.2. Bam Creative

When considering my own business name, I had a multitude of options. I liked the idea of incorporating my name in the business identity; however, I did want to leave my options open in case I ever hired staff.

Although my name (Miles Burke) is fairly unusual, the domain name milesburke.com was taken at the time, and I didn't want to tie it in so closely to me in any case.

My initials are MB or MAB in full, and I didn't believe these really stood out. However, when you reverse them, you end up with BAM, which I felt suggested impact. I knew that *Bam* was a very popular word, though, so I assumed there was no chance of getting those domains using it by itself.

Although most of my work at the time was web site design and development, I was occasionally brought in on corporate identity design or consulting projects. I'd already decided that I planned to stick to creative work, so I ended up choosing the business name Bam Creative.[3]

This allows my business to work on anything from web sites to logos and anything else that can be broadly considered creative, and still be true to the name. The word *Bam* is generic enough for most people never to make the connection that it's someone's initials, and certainly not the *reverse* of someone's initials!

Funnily enough, I did manage to register the domain bam.com.au, but I had no chance of getting any top-level domains (.com, .net or .org). Luckily, I got the full bamcreative business name versions of these.

Considering Your Business Structure

When setting yourself up as a business, you should consider the implications of different business structures. If you intend to take on staff within the first few years, you may wish to set up a corporation. If you plan to remain a solo worker, having everything set up as a sole proprietorship may be the best solution.

---

[3] http://www.bam.com.au/

Having said this, consider speaking to an accountant and possibly a lawyer to seek advice about your particular scenario. You could also speak to local business bureau (such as SCORE[4]) or associations. They'll take into account your current personal and financial situation, as well as your legal jurisdiction. Requirements for different business and company registrations will vary depending upon your location.

Each different structure can have a considerable impact on your taxation benefits, your licensing and governmental costs, and your ability to grow the business in the future.

The main differences between a **limited liability company** (an LLC) and a **sole proprietor arrangement** reside in the varying levels of possible taxation benefits, legal protection, ability to obtain finance, and your legal requirements.

Setting up an LLC structure has both advantages and disadvantages. The advantages include:

greater legal protection	If a client sues the company, only company assets can be seized to pay any judgement, not your own car or house.
greater ability to obtain credit	Many financial institutions and lenders have a preference for a company, rather than an individual, for business finance.
tax benefits	In some states and locations, a company receives more taxation benefits than a person.

This option isn't entirely free of disadvantages, of course. An LLC costs money to set up, and there are ongoing company-related fees. Also, financial reporting is usually more involved than for an individual.

Being in a sole proprietor structure has its fair share of benefits, mostly to do with cost. When compared with an LLC, there's less financial reporting for most situations, fewer start-up administration costs, and not as many licensing or business costs.

---

[4] http://www.score.org/

There are disadvantages though, which are easily recognizable as the other side of the LLC advantages:

zero legal protection If a client should sue you, the court can order that your assets be taken to pay any legal judgment.

less access to credit Business loans are likely to be harder to get for a sole proprietor than for an LLC.

tax burdens You may be taxed more than if you were a company.

Ideally, whatever structure you create now will mean that you aren't paying more than you need to in fees and costs, yet allow you to be flexible enough to accommodate change as your business and your direction evolve.

It's also a very good idea, regardless of your structure, to open a bank account for your freelance business that is separate from you as an individual. This way, you can pay yourself as if you were an employee, and allow a small nest egg to grow in the business account for those quieter months.

This account will also be used to pay all of your running costs, making the bookkeeping side of your new venture easier to manage.

Speak to as many other freelancers and small business owners as well, and ask them how they set up their own structure—people will soon tell you the pros and cons of their decisions, and this can save you a fortune in reorganization in the future.

Engaging Assistance

Early on in starting out on your own, you'll want to make alliances and choose suppliers for those services or products that you don't offer yourself.

A word from the wise: be very careful when choosing a supplier. Using a third-party product or service for a client project is akin to offering a raving endorsement about them, so it's important to consider your options before making your decision.

As your freelance business grows, you will find yourself using a multitude of suppliers. You'll find that whole areas of your business rely on them, and they in turn will benefit from the business that you bring them.

You'll need a domain name registrar, a hosting company, an office stationery supplier, a printer for business cards or other printed matter, and possibly an accountant or lawyer—or both. There will no doubt be other suppliers along the way. And then, of course, there's the large question of outsourcing—as we'll see, it's a false economy to spend time struggling to fulfil the complex requirements of thorough bookkeeping, to use a common example. There are experts to do it quickly and easily while you devote your time to the work at which you excel and that makes you money.

Spend any amount of time on web-based forums frequented by freelancers and you'll inevitably find discussion threads regarding freelance tales of woe—freelancers losing all of their data as a result of using the cheapest hosting company they could find, or having suppliers directly contact all of their clients, offering to undercut their best deals.

 Lessons Learned

Don't leave backups to your hosting provider. Regularly back up client sites, just in case—this may save you in the future!

If you're going to resell third-party services or products, ensure that you have a written contract stating what is acceptable and what isn't. The last thing you want is for your hosting company to go directly to your client base and offer them a great deal to cut you out of the picture.

Do some online research, and read up on the experiences other freelancers have had with the suppliers you have under consideration. Forums such as Web Hosting Talk[5] (see the Reseller Forum) and the SitePoint Forums[6] (see the Web Hosting Forums) have plenty of posts pertaining to which hosting companies treat their resellers well, and which don't.

The same approach applies to most suppliers you'll require—there are domain name registrar reviews, printing company reviews, and plenty of other sites and forums to be found.

---

[5] http://www.webhostingtalk.com/
[6] http://www.sitepoint.com/forums/

Once you have chosen a supplier, I encourage you to build a real rapport with them—a great relationship with a supplier can be worth a fortune in a time of crisis, or when you need something done absolutely drop-everything *now*.

Asking for Advice

One of the disadvantages of a freelance life is working in isolation. You won't have a team around you, and at times you may feel as though you're the last person on earth.

This is even more obvious when you realize you probably don't have someone to give advice. Sure, your partner or family can help to a degree, but they can't answer questions about your chosen profession in any great detail, unless web expertise runs in the family.

Look through your contacts, and see if you know someone who would be able or willing to play an informal mentoring role. You may be surprised as you look through your contacts on social networking sites or in your address book as to who could give you a hand; it's often even more surprising how willing people are to be helpful.

Look for freelance or web industry groups that have meet-ups. There are groups like Refresh,[7] Port80,[8] BarCamp,[9] web design meetups,[10] and more, where you can mingle with like-minded freelancers to share stories and ask for advice.

If there are no obvious candidates among your contacts and no local groups, make contacts through discussion forums and your extended networks, or even consider starting your own group. A buddy system between other freelancers, or with a mentor who's been doing the freelance or small business gig for a couple of years, can provide an invaluable sounding board and information source.

---

[7] http://refreshingcities.org/
[8] http://www.port-80.net/
[9] http://barcamp.org/
[10] http://webdesign.meetup.com/

Remember to Have Fun!

There may be times ahead that will make you feel overwhelmed by the mission that you've chosen to undertake—juggling money, being a salesperson, working late at night, and seemingly never stopping or being free of responsibility for your business.

However, make sure you take time to look at your achievements, the hurdles you've crossed, and the exciting road still in front of you. Freelancing is a rewarding career choice, and allows a level of flexibility that you've no doubt dreamed of.

Take time to have fun, pat yourself on the back regularly, and know that the start-up phase is the hardest part—it will become easier and more enjoyable as you travel along this path.

The Pick-me-up List

Keep a list of recent goals you've achieved on a sheet of paper stuck up near your desk. On those dark days when you feel like nothing is working, read the list and reaffirm your progress so far.

Case Study

Emily

For the last few weeks, Emily has spent a few hours most evenings reading up on business planning, and getting a grip on what she believes are her development areas around her business administration knowledge. Not only has she been furiously reading blogs and discussion forums on this subject, Emily has also managed to scour her local library for relevant books to read on the train.

Emily has written the shell of a plan, and as she makes decisions, she adds them to this file. Although she has some savings behind her, Emily is using spreadsheets to keep track of what expenses will crop up in the first three months, and is working to allow for them as soon as possible.

After much deliberation, she has decided since most of her work will actually come from other web companies and freelancers, and she is certain that she'll never have any staff working for her, that she'll use her name as her trading name. Emily has a friend who is a graphic designer, and she's asked him to work up her stationery in exchange for some web development work for one of his clients.

Jacob

Jacob has grand plans, and hopes to hire an office and employ staff within his first year. Since trialing a few names with friends, Jacob is down to two contenders, and has decided to spend a few weeks weighing them up before making a decision.

Meanwhile, he has surveyed a few friends about their hosting suppliers, and already has contacts at a local printer for when he is ready. A work colleague has offered to do the development for Jacob's web site, in exchange for cash.

Jacob is keen to start telling all of his contacts his plans, but also knows he needs to hand in his resignation first and get everything sorted—he's worried that when he tracks down some leads, he won't even have a business card ready to hand them.

Summary

It's been quite a whirlwind, taking in all the far-ranging subjects of this chapter as you prepare for the complexities of freelance life! The approach to getting the ball rolling is as simple as jotting down your thoughts into a simple business plan, and writing a short list of goals and milestones to work toward in the next few months.

We discussed putting some serious thought into naming your freelance enterprise, and preparing to spend some money on a few staple business purchases. You also need to consider your business structure; making bad decisions now could have long-term and possibly expensive repercussions in the future.

We dealt with looking for suppliers whom you can trust, and considered the benefits of handing the painful paperwork over to a professional who can do it better than you can, and probably cheaper too. It's also worth looking for someone who can be your informal coach or mentor—their advice will be invaluable to you.

Finally, remember to recognize your recent achievements and have fun!

Now to the thorny subject that lies behind all enterprise! In the next chapter, we're going to take a look at the lolly, spondulicks, moolah, greenbacks, cashola—in other words, money.

3

Manage Your Money

So you've jumped into freelancing, whether in whole, part, or still progressing through the planning phase. Now it's time to sort out that "F" word: finances. Money is a fraught area for many businesses, large *and* small, but it doesn't need to be. If you manage your finances properly and keep your books in order, the oft-dreaded chore of bookkeeping will soon become neither bewildering nor onerous. And if you can tick all the boxes of keeping the work coming through the door, clients happy, and deadlines under control, cash flow need never be a nightmare.

In this chapter, we'll focus on the basics of accounting, and we'll use some formulas to work out your expected costs. Then we'll calculate that all-important hourly rate.

We'll also discuss why cash flow is such an important consideration when managing your finances, and look at ways to keep problem debtors in the black. We'll look at the software you can use for keeping your finances under control, and discuss where you can enlist help to untangle your accounts, when you need to do so.

We'll check in with what goes on the real world when we chat with UK designer and seasoned freelancer Mark Boulton about his experiences, and look at leasing, loans, and insurance.

Read on to discover how to keep that accounting monster in check!

Accounting Basics

The following concepts may seem like common sense, but they're often overlooked in the excitement of pushing your freelance business off the ground. And we all know what will happen if you don't keep an eye on the finances—don't we?

cash flow

> The ideal incarnation of cash flow is an amount of cash coming in that's greater than the cash going out; to put it bluntly, this is what will allow you to keep freelancing. It's obvious that when the cash coming in is less than the cash you are spending, something has to change. However, there's actually more to it than money in, money out—timing can also play a crucial role.

salary

> In terms of paying yourself a realistic salary, you should not only pay yourself what you would be likely to earn if you were employed, but also factor in those hidden extras, such as pension or superannuation plans, dental and health benefits, and the like—and to allocate and deposit funds accordingly. This isn't the time to give yourself a grand raise, though—it is still vitally important that there is money in that business account.

profit

> You may think as long as you're earning a decent salary, then that's all you need. Not true—having even a small layer of profit on top of all of your expenses, including your own salary, is a very important tool to weather months where the finances dry up or some other disaster occurs.

insurance

> You cannot afford to go without insurance, even if you think you can avoid it. There are a plethora of insurance options, and your financial advisor can help you with these. You should consider such insurance as professional indemnity, business liability, and income protection. Should something unexpected occur, these plans could really save you a whole world of trouble.

Determining Your Costs

You'll no doubt have heard the old phrase "it costs money to make money," and as cliched as this may sound, it is overwhelmingly accurate when applied to freelancing. No matter how tight a rein you keep on your expenses, you'll find unexpected bills are a fact of business life. By providing your budgeted amounts with generous margins, you'll be better prepared to cope with an unexpected cost.

Perhaps you've already considered obvious items such as hardware or software, but have you thought about their cost of replacement, or their upgrade or replacement cycle? Say you have a $2,500 computer, which you plan to replace every three years. That's $834 per year to put aside, and don't forget to record the depreciation!

Then let's say you have an operating system, a creative design software suite, an accounting package, and an office application package. Maybe you'll upgrade to the latest version for just the design and office suite every year—you'll be putting aside around $1,100 per year just to do that!

Then you have a printer, with those expensive ink replacements, a scanner, a broadband router, and a few wireless network parts.

And it goes without saying that you should attempt to calculate costs that you may not need right now, but may crop up in the near future. For example, it's far better to allow for your tax return costs as you go, rather than scrambling for funds when tax time comes around.

Costs Checklist

First, create a spreadsheet with three columns: *Cost Category*, *Monthly Cost*, and *Annual Cost*. Then enter the applicable headings from the following example list to the *Cost Category*, and estimate your costs, being either monthly or annual. You can also download an example spreadsheet from this book's web site.[1] Feel free to add any other expenses that don't appear on this list (shown in Example 3.1), if you consider them relevant to your business.

---

[1] http://www.sitepoint.com/books/freelancer1/

Example 3.1. Costs Checklist Items

Office Costs

- rent (if you work from home, determine your percentage of home use and—with advice from your accountant—make this a percentage of rent or mortgage)
- furniture (desk, chair, bookshelves, and the like)
- signage (if any)
- electricity
- water
- cleaning

Equipment Costs

- hardware: desktop computer
- hardware: laptop computer
- hardware: printer
- hardware: phone handsets, answering machine, fax machine
- hardware: other (wireless routers, thumb drives, and so on)
- software: office package
- software: design and development suites
- software: accounting package
- software: other

Communication Costs

- mobile phone costs
- fixed telephone costs
- Internet access

Travel Costs

- vehicle maintenance
- fuel (speak to your accountant about keeping a log book)
- taxis
- airfares
- accommodation
- conference fees

- meals and entertaining

Consumable Costs
- printer ink
- stationery
- postage and couriers
- paper
- pens, pencils, staples ...

Marketing and Advertising Costs
- your own web site hosting
- press advertising
- phone book advertising
- other advertising: trade magazines, business cards and stationery, conference flyers

Miscellaneous Costs
- legal fees (these are normally incurred at the start, so spread them over two or three years)
- accounting fees (spread any start-up fees over two or three years, and then add ongoing fees)
- professional memberships
- subscriptions (magazines, online publications)

Insurance Costs
- health insurance
- professional insurance
- income insurance
- business insurance
- office insurance

Then, multiply the monthly costs by 12 to calculate your annual cost. We'll use these annual cost figures later in this chapter.

This spreadsheet can be updated throughout the year, to reflect the real costs. You can compare budget versus actual to see how close these figures came at the end of the first year of freelancing.

 The Cost of Software

Software licensing is an often-overlooked expense when freelancers first set up. Consider all the different packages you may need, and allow for these costs from the start. Don't forget to look at open source, freeware, and shareware software as another option where you can, as many of these are just as functional as their commercial counterparts.

Considering Insurance

Nobody ever plans to fall ill, or expects a client to take legal action, but these unfortunate situations do occur. Insurance is the only way to ensure that you minimize the impact of such unexpected trials.

Ask an insurance broker what types of insurance you may need to allow for, and ensure that you shop around. Some premiums can be as much as double the price of competing products that offer exactly the same cover.

Make sure that you understand what can and cannot be claimed, and that you have a complete understanding of your chosen insurance policy before you hand over your hard-earned cash. There's nothing worse than enduring an extended illness, only to find that your insurance provider won't cover your loss of income because of some small issue detailed in the fine print.

You will find that most insurance is 100% tax deductible as well, which makes this solution even more attractive to freelancers.

Obtaining Accounting Software

We'll discuss giving your accounting and bookkeeping to a professional in a moment, but you will want to be familiar with your own finances to some degree. We'll discuss the basic options of controlling your own finances here before deciding how much you should control and how much you hand over.

There are seemingly as many accounting software choices available as there are freelancers. You should speak to colleagues to find what they use, and search out reviews and tutorials for these packages online before making a commitment.

The feature sets and costs vary widely between all of the options on the market, and there's no easy decision in this area. Any basic accounting package should allow you to track items such as:

- Accounts Receivable
- Accounts Payable
- General Ledger
- Billing
- Stock or Inventory
- Purchase Orders
- Sales Orders

Most systems allow you to send an invoice or receipt as a PDF by email, as well as the old fashioned "print out and mail" method. Some of the newer versions also feature handy functions, such as time sheets (so you can input your hours directly into the system), mail merge (so you can use as a basic mailing list), and automated debt collections or reminders.

Here's just a handful of the different options available to you:

System Software

Quicken (http://www.quicken.com/)
Quicken has at least five versions of its product, ranging from the ultra-light starter edition to the premier edition, which integrates with banks, tracks investments, and more.

M.Y.O.B (http://www.myob.com/)
Within its four products, FirstEdge through to Premier, M.Y.O.B software includes payroll, time billing, inventory, and even a simple contact database.

Quickbooks (http://www.quickbooks.com/)
With 15 different suites, Quickbooks has everything from home finance tracking through to Retail, Accountant, and Payroll editions.

Web-based Software

Saasu (http://www.saasu.com/)

The most mature of the web-based finance offerings, Saasu rolls out new features regularly, and has tight integration with social networks, search engines, and CRM systems, as well as including all the regular software features.

Less Accounting (http://lessaccounting.com/)

The folks at Less Accounting make a point of saying they aren't some bloated accounting package provider; they tout themselves as "simple small business accounting software."

Freshbooks (http://www.freshbooks.com/)

The Freshbooks system is both an invoicing and time tracking system, with widgets available for desktop integration, sophisticated reports and integration with the big-name payment gateways.

Irrespective of which accounting package you choose, it's very important that you ask your accountant or bookkeeper for advice prior to purchasing software, and for support in setting up your initial accounts. This can avoid more complex and expensive situations from occurring later on, when these professionals need to export files for lodgment, or work on the accounts themselves.

Most packages allow fairly easy exporting of data, so you can email your files to your accountant for review or lodgment. Don't think that choosing the most feature-packed software is best either; this can easily bewilder you and cause more issues than simpler software.

Most up-to-date accounting packages can also reconcile directly to your bank account. Such features can save you countless hours and many headaches.

Hiring Professionals

If I only had room for three words in this entire chapter, they would be *hire a professional.*

An accountant or bookkeeper will bring your accounts under control much faster than you ever could, and they're very likely to save you money as well. Let's face it: we might be fantastic at with crafting standards-compliant XHTML, or designing very usable and nicely designed interfaces, but we aren't on this planet to be accountants or lawyers. This is exactly the reason that most accountants or legal experts don't design or build their own web sites—it's not in their range of competencies or interests.

When I first started out on my own, I was very conscious about not spending any more money than I absolutely needed to. This would mean that I would often wrestle with my own bookkeeping well into the night and on weekends, in order to keep the accounts up-to-date. I took the same approach with every other element of my newly created job; I didn't particularly like most of these extra chores, to be honest, and I wasn't great at some of them. I would either complete these tasks far slower than others would, or worse still, not do them at all.

One day, a wise friend asked me how long it took me to do my monthly accounts. When I explained that I spent most of every weekend on them, it was quickly pointed out that it was costing me hundreds of dollars in lost income, not to mention priceless and necessary downtime, to do the books badly. When we weighed up the billable rate per hour that I lost as a result of working on non-billable stuff instead of money-making projects, and then compared that to having a bookkeeper do in a couple of hours a task that took me all weekend, I quickly decided to loosen the purse strings the smart way.

Let's use a simplified example. Say you charge yourself out at $100 per hour, and it takes you an entire day to manage your books per month, then the actual cost to you is around $750, assuming you could bill yourself out for seven-and-a-half hours that day.

Now, you go to a local accountant or bookkeeper and ask them to do your monthly books at $50 per hour, and they take four hours. Not only have you saved yourself the headache of doing the work, you are over $500 better off, assuming you can fill that day with billable work.

If you're really lucky, you may find a professional nearby in the need of your services; both parties win if you can barter work with them!

It's worth having some awareness of your own finances, of course. However, the opportunity lost when you spend an entire day every fortnight on your accounts when you could be earning hundreds with billable work, should make sense straight away. If this isn't enough to convince you, consider your knowledge of accounting—do you feel satisfied that you know every single tax deduction and tax strategy to save you from paying more tax than you need to? Are you confident that you know a Profit and Loss statement in intimate detail?

If you have answered in the negative to either of these questions, do yourself a huge favor, and find a great accountant (ask for referrals from other freelancers, ask your bank manager or insurance broker, or ask industry and social contacts for referrals) who understand freelancers and can give you great advice.

If you are reasonably confident in your own abilities, perhaps you could ask for a quarterly or annual review. Regardless of the frequency, I urge you to seek professional financial opinion—regularly.

 ## Managing Your Money ... with a Little Help

One of the biggest reasons freelancers fail in their first year or two stems from their lack of financial planning and control. It can often feel overwhelming to manage your accounts, but without good management, the money could dry up.

Don't be hesitant to ask others for advice. There are plenty of online forums and web sites discussing money matters, and professional help from your accountant can make a world of difference.

You are not alone in facing these hurdles, so embrace opportunities for assistance from others who know accounting inside and out—it may save you from having to ditch freelance life and seek employment.

Making More Money ... with a Little Help

This may sound ridiculously obvious, yet we all suffer from letting ourselves become wrapped up in the detail. This trap means that we forget about the most important detail of all, which is to find out what makes us profitable so that we can repeat it.

We all have projects or tasks that we need to do regularly, but upon analyzing them in more detail, it's often clear that many of them waste time and make no profit. Or, even worse, end up making a loss. Stop doing them—hand them over to a professional!

It's hard as a freelancer to learn to say no, but if you don't, you can easily become caught in spending your time on less profitable activities. Get in the habit of regularly reviewing your time sheets and your income—discover where your real profit lies, and concentrate on that.

Calculating Your Rates

There are basically two ways in which most freelancers charge for projects. The traditional method of a "per project" fee is often referred to as a **fixed price contract**, while charging by the hour is often referred to as **time and materials**.

In either scenario, it is very important to work out what your minimum hourly rate should be. This way, you can track your progress against this minimum rate in the case of a project fee, or know what to charge as an hourly rate.

 Cover Yourself with Ad Hoc Loading

Project rates should be based on a minimum of your hourly rate multiplied by an estimation of hours involved, plus a loading to cover any ad hoc issues (which, depending on your previous experience with the client, you could anticipate to be large or small). This additional loading means that you will stay within budget more frequently, allows you to be more flexible with the occasional micro task or small scope creep, and helps avoid any issues at project completion.

Now, there are five steps to determine your hourly rate. You do this by looking at what it actually costs you to work per hour. There's a bit more to it than you might think ...

Step One: Determine Your Overheads

Using the spreadsheet you have created, you can now determine the annual costs per year, which we'll use in this calculation. It's prudent to add a further ten percent to this total, just to cover any unforeseen costs.

Step Two: Allocate Your Salary

There are a number of ways to calculate this figure, and you need to take into account your own particular expectations and lifestyle. However, a good yardstick is to look at what you could expect to be paid for doing the same work for an employer.

Perhaps you're already under employment, or have only recently left your job; if so, consider what your salary expectation would be in twelve months' time, including all taxes and employer contributions.

If you don't have this point of reference, look around a few employment-listing web sites and resources, or ask your peers in the business what they would consider to be a desirable salary for the work that you do.

Weigh up whether you wish to add a little more, to acknowledge that you're taking a risk in opting to work for yourself. This way, you really can create a desirable figure.

 Raise Your Rates!

As you would receive salary rises from time to time, you need to assess your billable rates in the same way—don't overlook the fact that as the years go by, your expertise grows, and therefore is worth more to the client.

Step Three: Decide on a Profit Margin

In all businesses, large and small, the aim of the game is profit. Being a freelancer should really be no exception. You'll want this margin for those times when cash flow is tight; moreover, by allowing for this profit now, you'll have some money saved for hiring staff or expanding the office when your business grows.

Step Four: Work Out Your Realistic Hours

Let's imagine for a moment that you could work 40 hours per week, just as a starting point. Theoretically, this means you have 52 weeks multiplied by 40, which comes to 2,080 hours per year.

Now, if you were an employee, you'd likely have a number of federal or public holidays (roughly 11 in United States, 10 in Australia, and 9 in the United Kingdom). Let's make this 10 days per year for the sake of the exercise.

Now, none of us likes the idea of being ill, but it's an inescapable fact of life; we'll allow a week off for sickness per year as well. And of course you realize and respect the importance of achieving work–life balance when freelancing, so you'll want to allow at least three weeks of vacation leave on top of it all.

So we have 52 weeks, minus two weeks for public holidays, one week for sick leave, and three weeks for holidays. This calculates to 46 weeks of actual work, or 1,840 hours if we work 40 hours per week.

It is unrealistic to imagine that you are able to charge out all 40 hours in a week, if that's the sum total of the time you spend working. There are a number of un-chargeable tasks, such as administration, sales, meetings, travel, lunches, and other duties that will crop up in the best-run business.

A conservative estimate for these duties might reduce your billable hours by a further 25%, leaving you with 1,380 hours of billable work per year.

Step Five: Calculate Your Hourly Rate

Armed with the information from the four points before, we can now apply the following formula to create your hourly rate:

```
Pre-tax hourly rate =
(Annual Overheads + Expected Salary + Profit) / Billable Hours
```

For example, let's say we calculated $20,000 in overheads plus $40,000 salary, and we'd like a 10% profit margin; we divide $66,000 by 1,380 hours, which equates to $47.83 per hour.

Now that isn't the end of the equation. We may have a (fairly) scientifically calculated figure, but what we need to do now is to compare this against the range of rates in your local industry, and determine whether it is competitive.

For some people, keeping an hourly rate within a so-called industry standard may not be a concern—perhaps you're very specialized, or serve a niche market—but for most freelancers, it can make all the difference to landing those prospects who are shopping around. We all know that that deciding on hourly rate alone is a false economy on the part of the prospect, given that the amount of hours one person takes to complete a task could be five times greater than someone else, but we also know that most clients don't see it that way, especially if they're unfamiliar with using services such as yours.

 Selling Ahead

> Consider selling prepaid maintenance (perhaps in five-hour blocks), which is a nice means of immediate payment, and is a great way to cover incidental support requests.

Do some research into similar freelancers in your area in order to nail down a range of rates. Find out from colleagues what they charge, ask people who have used freelancers before, or ask a friend to obtain quotes from your competitors. Where does your rate fit in?

Is it cheap?

> This is a good situation to be in. You now have an opportunity to raise your hourly rate, and earn more income. You don't want your hourly rate to be significantly less than others, as it may make prospective clients start to wonder why you are so cheap, and doubt your abilities.

Don't Be Cheap

Don't, whatever you do, try to win work by being the cheapest. This devalues your work, does your wider industry no favors, and means you'll have a tougher time convincing clients of your value when you start raising your rates.

Many freelancers undercharge when they start, due to a lack of confidence or because they haven't considered all of their outgoings. You are taking this leap because you're worth it, so don't cave into that inner demon of self-doubt!

Is it middle of the range?

Well done! This is the sweet spot—there are freelancers who charge more than you, yet you aren't in the bargain basement, either. This is the price area that most freelancers should really aim for in their first few years.

Is it higher than average?

If your rate is higher than most, you need to look at what the factors are. You don't want to be the cheapest; however, being the most expensive may make life a little tougher, if you're finding clients resistant to the idea.

Review all of your figures from above. Did you exaggerate any overheads too far? Have you added a very large profit percentage? If so, perhaps you need to consider tuning down slightly, to make your rate more realistic and attractive.

Many freelancers complain that people new to freelancing attempt to attract clients by offering considerably cheaper rates. This practice ends up representing a danger to these newbies rather than the freelancers whom they undercut, as they've very likely failed to consider their overheads sufficiently. The bright side for seasoned and reasonably priced freelancers is that their fresh-faced competitors may not be freelancing for very long! The unfortunate aspect, however, is that this situation can cause other freelancers to panic and reduce their pricing, thereby creating a spiral towards low costs and a resultant reduction in quality.

Don't get caught up in the same game—it's far better to stick to your guns and maintain that you need to be reasonable in your charges, so that you can assure clients you'll still be freelancing in a year to come.

Also remember that not *all* new clients shop around. In some situations, it may be common to find that a prospect has had no other quotes than your own, before they make a decision in your favor. This will often become evident during the sales process.

Bartering Your Skills

To increase your billable hours, consider outsourcing your low-paying, repetitive tasks to allow you to focus more time on the more specialized work you excel at. Smarter still, find a freelancer with better skills in server administration, and arrange to swap services, such as your legendary proficiency in graphics preparation. They'll be quicker at their area of expertise, and vice versa, so both parties win!

Cash Flow Is King!

Let's look at the first concept we met at the very start of this chapter in more detail: operational cash flow. You may feel great sending out all those invoices; however, those sheets of paper won't help pay your expenses. The proof is in the payments—and it's when they actually arrive in your bank account that matters. As we'll discuss, not all businesses are keen to abide by your terms of payment.

When funds are tight, it's imperative that you do what you can to balance the income and outgoings so that you'll always have money available in the bank. It's a good practice to adopt from the very start, and continue into the future.

You should concentrate your efforts on:

reducing the average collection period
This is the time that lapses between the invoice going out, and the payment being received.

reducing the risk of bad debtors
Nobody likes the idea that some clients may never pay!

budgeting for future expenses
It's probably not necessary to buy that shiny new gizmo right now. Create a cash flow plan, and determine the best time to make a purchase.

timing your outgoing payments
Ensure that you have a credit period with purchases, and that you use this wisely.

It isn't just when you're beginning your freelance career that cash flow is such a crucial element. Ask any business owner, and they'll agree that controlling cash flow is an ongoing challenge—the failure of which can cripple any organization, whatever the size.

Three Types of Cash Flow

There are three types of cash flow in business. **Operational cash flow** is cash received or spent for a core business activity. This is the type of cash flow most applicable to freelancers.

Financing cash flow is cash received or expended as a result of financial activities, such as interests or dividends. **Investment cash flow** is cash received or spent on investments, acquisitions, and capital expenditure. The latter two are typically not so relevant to freelancers.

Encouraging Prompt Payment

One of the biggest issues that many freelancers face is being paid on time. The consequences of waiting months for a large bill to be settled—especially when it's payment for a job that took up all your resources for a significant period of time and prevented you from taking on smaller fry to keep you going—can be severe. You need to be prepared for such eventualities as best you can, with enough savings and cash flow to tide you over.

It's often the case that the larger the organization, the quicker their clients pay, due to the fact that larger organizations employ people to chase down their debtors. Unfortunately, these larger organizations are also typically the ones that are slowest at paying their own bills.

You can encourage prompt payment from clients by using a number of strategies. Ensure that you invoice as frequently and as quickly as possible. You can arrange milestone payments at the start, during the project, and at the end. Smaller invoices are normally far more palatable than larger ones, so invoice early and often.

Ensure you cover every detail on your actual invoice, so that you minimize queries. These details should not only cover all of your legal and contact information, but also explain the charges and provide a brief description of the work, as well as the date incurred, if it's maintenance or support. Most importantly, ensure that your payment terms are clearly stated and are obvious to the recipient. Consider making them big and bold. For a sample freelance invoice, see this book's web site for a downloadable example.[2]

Find out the name of the person in the accounts department, and address the invoice accordingly. This way, there should be no excuses about the paperwork going astray or not being addressed to the person with the right authority. If you don't have any luck with the accounts people, politely mention it to the person or people you're dealing with on the project, if it's ongoing. They may be able to get the wheels in motion to ensure your willing continuation with the project, and to keep the relationship sweet.

Communicate frequently, and with consistency. If the invoice was due yesterday, email or call the client today and politely ask when payment will be received. Take a note of their response, and set a reminder to call again close to the date they nominated. Clients will quickly learn that if the account is still outstanding on the due date, they can expect a call from you.

Avoid setting unrealistic payment terms. Many companies will simply ignore payment terms if they are less than 14 days. Similarly, they will sit back and wait for a statement or follow-up if you give 90-day terms. Find a nice window (I typically use 30 days) which most clients will stick to, and avoid changing your payment terms for difficult clients, without a very good reason (or additional loading!).

---

[2] http://www.sitepoint.com/books/freelancer1/

Discounting to Save Headaches

Some businesses and freelancers offer a small discount if the invoice is paid by a certain date, or is prepaid. I'm not a big fan of this approach, but many other freelancers report considerable success this way. My main concern with offering this carrot is that you could open yourself to arguments when a client pays *after* the due date, but still insists upon receiving the discount that they now look upon as your expected, standard rate.

Dealing with Debtors

When faced with a debtor who just isn't paying up, there's always a temptation to inflame the situation by pulling out that jousting equipment beloved of our freelance forebears. Don't! Approaching the situation with discourtesy, aggression, or threats simply won't work; it will only escalate the issue into a personal grudge and bring any negotiations to a standstill.

The best approach is to be firm about your expectations and agreements, and ensure that you present this message in a written form. Inquire about the delay in payment with the person you've been dealing with, ask about whether there are any issues, and see what you can do to resolve them.

If absolutely necessary, agree on a payment plan—even though this won't help your short-term money needs, it's better to at least have a trickle of the money coming in than no money at all. And you'll often find that the mere insinuation that a client can't pay their bills will lead to them paying up in order to save ego.

If there's still no resolution, consider engaging a debt collection agency—typically, they will take a percentage fee from the overall invoice, if they're successful in collecting the sum owed to you. In my opinion, it's better to salvage 80–90% of the total cost than none at all.

When You Need to Get Tough

An important consideration is that debts become harder to recoup the longer they exist, so it's vital to act quickly with recalcitrant clients. If all negotiations fail, look at options such as locking troublesome clients out of their CMS, delaying any remaining work until they have paid you in full for your work to date, or as an absolute last resort, turning off their web site hosting.

Recurring Revenue

Regardless of whether you're charging by the project or by the hour, an income stream that shouldn't be overlooked is that of **recurring revenue**, also known as "passive income."

Let's consider a quick example. Say we bought hosting accounts for $12 per month, and we could sell them to our clients for $20 per month. But, you might say, that's a whole $8. It's not going to change *my* life!

Well, what about an average of two clients a month signing up for your hosting? This means that after two years, you will have 48 sites hosted on your reseller hosting account. This works out to a rather nice $384 per month—for doing very little.

Now, let's add domain names, secure certificates, and other add-on items into this equation, and I'm sure you'll really start to see value in the proposition.

Can you build a web application? An important opportunity for those who create products, such as content management systems or web apps, is to reduce any upfront costs of the installation—which therefore makes it more affordable and attractive—and build in an annual, recurring licensing fee. This is an example of the power in numbers—ten clients paying $200 a year for CMS licensing means an extra two thousand dollars per year in passive income.

This principle isn't just for hosting, domain names, and applications, of course. There's a multitude of items from which you can create products, and sell over and over again. Consider such items as membership sites, advertisement-funded sites (a successful blog is a good example), or sales of photographs and illustrations on stock design sites such as iStockPhoto[3] and BigStockPhoto.[4]

Then there's writing an ebook for sale, designing T-shirts and other designer items and selling them through sites such as RedBubble[5] and Spreadshirt,[6] developing web-based applications, or even creating web site design templates for sale.

Loans and Savings

At the very least, you should have a bank account created solely for your business use. Don't blur the line between your money and your business's money, as it can allow you to fall into the trap of spending everything that you make.

Organize a main business bank account, and then draw on that account for your own wages—a weekly or fortnightly transfer to another personal account does the trick.

Then, ensure that a percentage of the income being deposited into this business account is never touched. This will allow a small amount to grow into something that can be used for larger capital expenses down the track, such as a new laptop or color laser printer.

It's also wise to consider having yet another account for items that need to be paid regularly but infrequently, such as taxes and superannuation—this way, when tax time comes, you won't need to struggle to find the money. Work out what income tax rate you'll most likely need to pay, and consider automatic transferral of that percentage from any income into this account.

Don't be shy about applying for a loan to help sort out your start-up costs. Many people find it very hard to fund the costs of starting up from the meager income they make in those first few months. It's a shame for lack of funds to hold you back, if you have to turn down projects because you don't have the right software or hardware, and it's probably avoidable if you have a decent credit history. It's crucial, of course, to make sure that you can meet the repayments.

---

[3] http://www.istockphoto.com/

[4] http://www.bigstockphoto.com/

[5] http://www.redbubble.com/

[6] http://www.spreadshirt.com/

If you do get a loan at any stage, make sure that the loan is serviced from your business account, and treat it as a company expense. Blurring the line between personal and business money will cause headaches at tax time, and adds unnecessary complexity to your bookkeeping.

Interview with Mark Boulton

Mark Boulton is a graphic designer based in Cardiff, UK. He used to work as Art Director for Agency.com, and as a Senior Designer for the BBC, before starting his own design consultancy, Mark Boulton Design Ltd.[7] With over ten years of design experience, Mark primarily works on the Web, although he's partial to a bit of print every now and then.

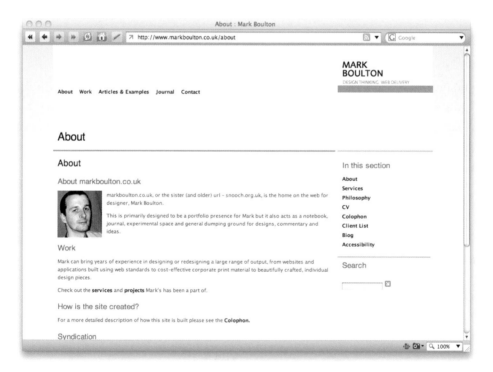

Figure 3.1. Mark Boulton's web site (http://www.markboulton.co.uk/)

---

[7] http://www.markboultondesign.com/

I recently spoke with Mark Boulton about his money management techniques:

What methods do you use to manage the finances of your business?

For the annual and monthly finances, I have a good accountant who provides me with a bookkeeper who comes in every month to post bank reconciliations and sales invoices—all that sort of thing.

For the day-to-day, I've started using an online application called Less Accounting.[8] This has all the essentials I need: invoicing, proposals, VAT reports, and so on.

Do you have strategies to manage cash flow, and if so, what are they?

In addition to Less Accounting—which helps visualize the current state of cash flow—I basically use a bunch of lists in Backpack.[9] I have daily, monthly, and quarterly lists. The monthly ones usually deal with which client needs to be invoiced during the month and for what value. The quarterly list details the three-monthly amounts to see if I'm on track for targets.

It's a really basic system, but in three years (two of those years full-time), I've looked at—and rejected—a lot of systems that are supposed to help with cash flow. To be honest, nothing has come close to having these lists. I've found cash flow is such a fluid thing that you need the freedom within an application or system to move things around as much as you want, without being bogged down by features you'll never use.

If there was one money tip you could give for freelancers starting out, what would it be?

Check your bank account a lot. Before I went into business, I was a little scared of checking my balance. I was hopeless with money—I'd just rather ignore the problem. Well, it's the worst thing you can do. Keep a very close eye on where you are with your cash; what's owed, by whom, and when do you expect to receive it.

---

[8] http://www.lessaccounting.com/
[9] http://www.backpackit.com/

The moment an invoice is late, chase it. Then continue to chase it every few days until you receive payment. Make yourself in a thorn in the debtor's side—they'll pay you to shut you up, and that's just fine!

Case Study

Emily

After considerable thought, Emily has decided to keep to the lower end of her rates calculations, at least at the start, while she gets her name in at larger web companies and targets some select clients.

Emily has created a second bank account, and has put her savings into it, as a "loan" to herself. This way, she can keep an eye on what she has spent in the set-up phase.

She's using a web-based accounting system and has bought a few books on accounting, to familiarize herself with the basics. Emily has decided that she'll run her accounts past a bookkeeper for review at least once a year.

At this stage, it's all about keeping a lid on money, now that she's made the leap and has to live on a tight weekly budget.

Jacob

Jacob knows he doesn't have the patience or inclination to manage accounts all the time, so he's wangled a swapping-services deal to build a web site for a bookkeeper friend.

Jacob has finally left his employer, and he's spending all his time working on his networks. As much as he'd like to learn the intricacies of balance sheets, forward projections, and budget forecasting, he's beginning to realize that it may be best to just leave it to the experts for now.

Jacob has spent a fair amount on new equipment, borrowing $3,000 from his family to do so, but he's confident he can pay it back within 18 months. In order to borrow the money, he had to prove to his parents that he has a business plan and has the appropriate insurance—this outlay was considerably less than what the bank wanted to charge to loan him the money he needed.

Summary

We started out this chapter by discussing the basics of accounting. After some soul-searching and not-too-heavy mathematical formulas, we ascertained your likely costs before calculating your hourly rate.

We covered a lot of ground, but there are a few points to remember as you continue on this journey. Cash flow is absolutely vital for success. If there's no income, there's no money for jousting equipment.

There's a number of ways to encourage prompt payment—use them all to ensure clients stay on track. Don't be afraid to confront problem debtors—do you really want a long-term client who never pays their bills anyway?

It's a time for being careful with money going out. Look at leasing and bank loans as options for paying for large ticket items now. That said, there are a few expenses you should accept rather than try to do without. Insurance is a must, as well as great accounting software. Hiring a bookkeeper or accountant is one of the key simple strategies to keep on top of those books and money juggling.

Finally, don't forget to ask for help if you need it—professional advice will get you sorted in very little time!

In the next chapter we'll look at what you need to get started in freelancing.

Chapter

4

Set Yourself Up

To be a successful freelancer takes hard work and a focus on productivity. Sort yourself out with a desk and chair, the right software, and a good working environment, and you've taken the first steps to achieve that success.

In this chapter, we'll consider the best location for your home office, the basics of ergonomics, and the importance of keeping leisure and work on separate sides of the fence.

Then, we'll touch on maintaining your health, take a look at strategies of time tracking and scheduling, discuss the subject of personal productivity, and check out some online tools you may want to consider using in your freelance life.

We'll also deal with those all-important legal contracts, look at the benefits of software licensing, and finish up this chapter on the subject of data backups.

Planning Your Office Space

The space in which you do your work may have a larger impact on your productivity than you'd care to admit. If you've made the decision to work from home—as do the largest proportion of freelancers—you need to ensure that you equip and plan the space well.

Even if you have to begin freelancing from the kitchen table or a local cafe, many of these points remain relevant, although you may have restricted opportunities to change the physical environment to such a large degree.

Many modern homes already have an allowance for a home office, and this is an obvious choice. Otherwise, perhaps you have a spare room such as a bedroom or under-utilized living space?

You need to take into account a number of factors when preparing your work space. You can't always have everything, of course, but here are a few questions to consider, which are highly pertinent to setting up a home office:

Is it quiet and free of interruptions?

Look carefully at the issues of privacy and being able to work in uninterrupted quiet—the living room or other main thoroughfare may not be the best choice if you live with others. A better location would have the simple facility of closing the door, allowing you to physically separate the working and personal spheres of your home.

Is the temperature pleasant, and do you have a fresh air source?

These considerations fall down in many home offices, such those situated in a shed or extension never designed for eight hours a day of habitation. You don't want to find yourself reluctant to enter or remain in a space that bakes you in summer and freezes you in winter. A working space with fresh air helps prevent you suffering from sleepiness due to the room being too warm and stuffy—if you don't have access to fresh air, consider installing a slow-moving portable or ceiling fan to provide some decent airflow.

Does the room have a window—and even a view?

Besides providing natural light, many people like to occasionally stare off into space out the window, to relax the eyes and provide a meditative break during the course of the day. Staring at a blank wall all day is both boring and not very healthy; being too close to the wall also doesn't allow you to exercise your eyes and can cause eyestrain or fatigue.

Does it have adequate utilities access?

You'll need a number of power points, access to a phone line, and possibly data points or a wireless network as well. It's fantastic to have access to a comfortable spare bedroom, but you're asking for trouble if you don't have enough power, phone, and data points available—as is often the case in rooms not designed to be offices. Running a number of devices all from one power socket is a serious health and safety risk, let alone a potential disaster for work not backed up—call an electrician to come in and add some more points around the room.

Do you expect to have clients drop in?

If so, how will you walk them from the front door to your desk or meeting space? It can often feel invasive to have a client traipse through your living room or kitchen to reach your office space. If you'd rather avoid having clients enter your home, or fear that you may look unprofessional, consider hiring a conference room or boardroom—they are fairly inexpensive if you only have the occasional meeting, and it's often a more professional-looking alternative. More casual options might include your local cafe, which has the bonus of being free and providing great coffee!

Figure 4.1. Plan your home office location carefully

Once you've chosen a space, it's time to furnish it with the essentials. I suggest you start off small and add to the room over time, rather than spending thousands only to find you don't really use all that furniture, much as that antique drafting table appealed to you at the time. Decide how much you can afford to start with, and stick to it—even if it prevents you from buying that $5,000 Swedish-designed office chair you were coveting!

As a bare minimum, you'll need a suitably large desk, a comfortable and ergonomically sound chair (more on this shortly), some filing space (a cabinet or even a few box files are usually sufficient), a bookshelf for related books and folders, and space for a phone, printer, and possibly a fax machine.

Visit local salvage stores, auctions, or even sites such as eBay for office furniture; you can normally grab a bargain, and often they need merely a good clean and perhaps a lick of paint to look fine.

You may want to also consider adding a lamp or new lighting, depending on the current light sources. Lighting is an important component of saving your eyes from fatigue. You should have more than just the light from your monitor illumining your room, and avoid backlighting from a window or other strong light source directly behind the monitor. A good desk lamp and maybe some surrounding up-lights for diffused lighting are perfect for an office.[1]

 Cheap Green Lighting

Replace your traditional incandescent light bulbs with energy-efficient compact fluorescent ones. Not only are they great for the environment, they can save some serious money; they use 80% less electricity and last nine times longer than traditional globes. Again, it's a good idea to balance any fluorescent glare with a halogen desk lamp.

And finally, remember that the ideal work environment is warm and friendly—but not *too* comfortable. You're in it to work, not sit back and relax, so resist the

---

[1] For a couple of excellent sources on saving your eyesight in the office, see http://www.ipnlighting.com/blog/2007/02/22-ways-to-reduce-eye-strain-at-your.asp and http://www.scif.com/safety/OfficeLighting.html.

temptation of locating a TV, games console, or other likely distraction in the same room.

Considering Ergonomics

Most freelancers typically work long hours at a stretch. This is the main reason that freelancers sometimes suffer from sore lower backs, headaches, and blurred vision. You can avoid these nasty side effects by being considerate to your body and aware of good ergonomics.

One major example of considering ergonomics when setting your office up lies in your choice of chair. A great office chair has adjustable height, and an adjustable backrest which you can bring into the small of your back, as well as tilt back and forth. Tilting the seat and back of your chair forward slightly reduces strain on the lower back and encourages better posture. The seat should be short enough to allow you full back support without digging into the back of your knees, and well padded.

Figure 4.2. Invest in a great office chair

Choose a desk that's large enough for most items, but that doesn't require awkward stretching to get to frequently used items, such as phones. Consider an L- or U-shaped desk, as these models offer more desk space without the need to move your chair.

The height of the desk in relation to your chair should allow you to set your monitor up by centering it slightly below eye level, and about an arm's length from your seated position. Monitors can easily be raised using books or a stand. This will allow you to keep your head on a comfortable angle and minimize glare.

If you use a laptop, consider having a laptop stand and a separate keyboard. The stand raises the laptop screen to the correct height, while the keyboard allows you to place the screen the correct distance from your seat.

Ensure that you develop the habit of a good sitting posture. It's all too easy to kick off the shoes and lie back in the chair as though you're flying a jet fighter; not great for your back. You need to keep your feet in contact with the floor, your elbows and arms at a good angle, and your head and neck straight. If your neck feels uncomfortable or strained at the end of a few hours of work, you'll likely need to adjust the height of your monitor.

You've possibly seen those funky workout balls that some people sit on, and you may consider trying those—they can help develop good posture and back support, because you need to utilize those core muscles to stay balanced, rather than slumping in a chair. It's best to take a moderate approach to changing the seating habits of a lifetime; 20-minute sessions are probably enough to begin with. The same goes for the ergonomic kneeling chairs without backs—these keep your hips and knees at the ideal angle to automatically shift your frame's balance to protect your lower back and encourage a more upright posture, but they can take time to grow comfortable with for long periods of sitting. Think about seeking advice from your local specialist office furniture store—many of these have lots of experience with setting up ergonomic office environments. It's a good idea to consult a chiropractor or osteopath regularly, and even pay the occasional visit to an optometrist; these professionals can not only suggest ways to set up your desk and chair to suit your frame, but also provide exercises to suit your needs.

Research desk-based exercises, such as neck stretching and eye focusing. Although these exercises are typically only a few minutes in duration, they are good for breaking up the day. And try to stand up and move about once a hour, even if only to fetch yourself a glass of water or use the bathroom—the short walk stimulates oxygen and blood flow.

 Remind Yourself to Take a Break!

Set a reminder that will alert you every hour to have a short break. Even just standing up and stretching can avoid Repetitive Strain Injury (RSI), encourage better blood circulation, and revive you in such a way that you'll be more productive. Try working in blocks: work an hour, take a five-minute break; work another hour, and take a longer break.

If you find your wrist or the back of your hand aching after long periods of typing, consider some form of wrist support; there are ergonomic mousepads available with wrist padding, often gel or dense foam. And if you use the phone a lot, make sure you avoid one of the worst habits office workers fall into—instead of crunching your neck as you support the receiver between your head and shoulder, consider buying a hands-free headset or handset bracket.

Separating Work and Life

Having clear boundaries between your work and your life may sound like a no-brainer, but it can often prove to be a real challenge for new freelancers bursting with enthusiasm and feeling obliged to take on any work that's available. This separation, however, it is a habit to encourage from the start. You may feel internal pressure to work long hours and burn the midnight oil, but lack of rest and downtime just makes you less productive in the long run.

Think of the division of work (the time your spend on building business and doing the work) from life (you know, that other stuff: shopping, eating, family time, and other non-work activities). I'm not talking about physical barriers when I say this, but there are some physical elements to this process too. For instance, as mentioned earlier in this chapter, ensure that your "office" doesn't consist of a couch in front of a television or the latest games console. As well as only serving to distract you, this practice also blurs the boundaries between work and play.

Achieving a balance between working and non-working time will actually increase productivity, not diminish it. If you can start creating some barriers between the two right now, while you are just starting off on this adventure, you're setting yourself up for a healthy outlook. This needn't be a strict 9.00 a.m. to 5.00 p.m. division; you may find your optimum work time is in the afternoons. You can certainly start your day at 11.00 a.m. and work through to 7.00 p.m. if this arrangement best suits your particular mode of productivity, but try to stick to it.

For a change of scene, try visiting a local cafe or library with a free wireless hotspot. This can provide some much-needed human interaction. If the external noise is an issue, take some headphones along and listen to some music suitable to work by (and only you can determine what constitutes this!) from your laptop.

If you need a landline, it's a good idea to organize a second telephone line for your home office, and to remove any handsets associated with the home line from your workspace; you don't need the distraction of telemarketers or mothers-in-law. The same goes for answering the front door; unless you're expecting a client, ignore that doorbell.

You might like to install some speakers in your room, so you can play some background music; this can help block out what's going on in the rest of the house, muffle the next-door kid's trombone practice, or even hide that eerie silence as you work away on your own.

Now to your attire. Your first attraction to a freelance lifestyle may have been the prospect of spending all day in your fleecy pajamas, but you'd be better off to wake up at a reasonable hour each day, shower and dress though you're indeed leaving to go to a workplace, and bid goodbye to the other occupants of your home before retiring to your office. Of course, you don't need to don a suit or dress to impress, unless you have a client meeting that day, but there can be a huge variation in attitude between muddling about in something you wouldn't answer the door in to dressing neatly and comfortably, and generally looking and feeling good.

Your partner, family, or friends may assume that, since you work for yourself, you have endlessly flexible time. They might take this as an opportunity to ask you to do the shopping, watch the kids, drop in for morning tea, and so on. Avoid this situation—be upfront with them and ask that they respect your work time as exactly that.

It is super-important, though, to take breaks such as lunch. If you have an outdoor area or park nearby, making your lunch and sitting outside is an excellent way to clear your head and mentally prepare for the next few hours. If you don't have access to such a retreat, or the weather forbids it, that's fine—just don't get too comfortable on the couch!

If you are really feeling isolated in your new lifestyle, try visiting a fellow freelancer, and work from their house for a day—although it may not be as productive as you'd hope, at first, the additional contact and creativity can provide a real boost to your enthusiasm.

You may find at times you need to work an extra few hours every day due to deadlines, horror projects, and similar pressures—that's fine, and you may want to reward your efforts by taking some breaks during these stressful moments, but be aware that spending half the day on Facebook or Twitter or playing online games is not going to help reduce these hours.

 Taking Care of Your Health

It's crucial that you take care of yourself physically, and although we'll cover this topic in more depth in Chapter 7, it's worth emphasizing the importance of your health here.

One of the big killers of personal productivity is being unwell. Invest some time to take regular walks, meditate, play team sport, or allow time for whatever stress-relieving exercise habit suits you best.

A happy and active person is a far more productive person, so don't end up creating a bad lifestyle for yourself.

Don't forget, even in those marathon coding or design shifts, to eat healthily and take regular breaks; this can save you from sick days off work later. Don't be afraid to invest in the luxury of the afternoon power nap, or even take an afternoon or morning off once in a while—well-earned breaks can improve your health and help avoid the consequences of having to lose a whole week because you've allowed yourself to become run-down and susceptible to illness.

Tracking Your Time

One of the most useful habits to adopt as quickly as you can is time tracking. Being aware of the fine details of how your days and nights are spent means that you can use this information to reflect on budgets versus actual hours, as well as bill for those hourly rate projects and tasks.

One of the greatest benefits of tracking hours is that it opens your eyes to how long a job *really* takes. It's one matter to say it takes you four hours to install a CMS or design a sleek user interface, but it's quite another when you add in the actual client contact time, the emails, the phone calls, the revisions … and if you follow the details, you'll quickly find where you underestimate.

A common beginner's mistake is to forget to include the administration time of the sales process; writing proposals, refining the documentation, and meeting with the client are legitimate hours, which should be included in your project hours. Using the information you collect from time tracking in future estimations ensures that you'll recover the real costs of doing the work, and be far more confident in determining what investment of time makes you money, and what drains it.

There are many methods to recording your time; these can range from keeping paper time sheets or using a spreadsheet to utilizing the calendar feature on your email suite; however, all of these options still require much manual processing before being able to tally and bill clients and projects.

Over the last few years, an explosion of web-based applications have appeared that can do this task for you. Many of them also have widgets for your computer desktop to book time and collate data.

Here are just a few of them:

Harvest (http://www.getharvest.com/)
> offers a limited free plan through to paid monthly plans; enables expense planning, quote tracking, invoicing, and many other accounting features

Tick (http://www.tickspot.com/)
> a simple time tracking system with RSS project tracking, reporting, Basecamp integration, and more

88Miles (http://www.88miles.net/)
> offers time budgeting, Saasu integration, project and shift tagging, as well as other great features

Basecamp (http://www.basecamphq.com/)
> so much more than time tracking; a full-blown project management system, with nice time-clocking and reporting features

Scheduling Your Time

The task of scheduling covers a wide array of duties. First, you have your effective working hours, which may not be the nine-to-five model to which, seemingly, the rest of the world works. You have the day-to-day scheduling of "stuff to do," and then you have the week-to-week or month-to-month project work with various milestones and stop/start points.

One of the payoffs for being a freelancer is the opportunity to dictate your own hours. You may be a morning person; perhaps you could start at 6.00 a.m. and finish the day in the middle of the afternoon. Or perhaps you're a night owl, and it may suit you to start at lunchtime and work through to eight or nine in the evening.

Ensure that you communicate your working hours to your clients; you'll find many will expect you to be at their beck and call from 8.00 a.m. through to 6.00 p.m. or even later. As suggested briefly in Chapter 1, it's best to have at least half of your working hours coincide with business hours, rather than beginning work at seven in the evening and finishing in the small hours of the morning, so that your clients grow frustrated that they can't get in contact with you when they try to call in your off-time. Whatever option you decide, it's a good idea to try to make it a regular time period every workday. This way, you can schedule the rest of your life (and don't forget to have a life!) around this shift at the coalface.

Then you have the daily tasks. I tend to use my own time management process here, and not become too caught up in scheduling blocks of time, unless they are for meetings; I use my email program's calendar tool exclusively for this.

Don't forget to allow time in your schedule for research and learning; this is often ignored when buried in your own work every day. When it comes to longer blocks of time, such as for large projects, the simplest scheduling tool is to use a whiteboard or wall planner to mark columns and rows, and use these for dates and project names. Factor in blocks of time for the larger projects every day, which allows you to fill the remaining time with the smaller work. This provides a very quick at-a-glance summary of your current workload. The downside is that it isn't very mobile, so you'll be stuck if you ever work from remote locations, such as a cafe or client office.

A similar tool can be your calendar in your email program. Microsoft Outlook, for example, can display a day, week, or month at a time, in an easy-to-digest layout, and the benefit here is that reminders and meeting requests can be sent and received by email and saved to your schedule easily. Many popular web applications also have calendar functions; perhaps your requirements can be met by a tool as accessible as Google Calendar.[2]

Don't get too caught up in designing the process, or spend big on software tools that are overblown with project features and not focused on simple scheduling; you'll soon find your rhythm and stick to it.

Discovering Your Personal Productivity

All freelancers discover within their first year or so that being busy and being productive can be oceans apart. Slaving away at your desk from dawn to midnight doesn't guarantee that you're being overly productive.

Searching the Web for productivity articles will likely make you think that a third of the Internet is dedicated to this subject; you'll read a lot of advice, some good, some average, but all worth considering, depending on your situation.

Here are my own favorite productivity tips:

Track your time.
> We're all guilty of short-changing our own expectations of how long a task or project will take. Track your time and review it constantly—the data this yields not only means you'll invoice the real hours now, but it also helps to protect you from under-quoting in the future.

Keep a to-do list.
> Use pen and paper, email yourself a list a few times per day, or just have a text file on your desktop. There are even online systems such as Ta-da List[3] or

---

[2] http://www.google.com/calendar/
[3] http://www.tadalist.com/

Remember the Milk[4] that can track your tasks. No matter how you approach it, a to-do list is invaluable.

Keep your workspace organized.

I'm not just talking about just your physical desk surrounds—keeping your computer desktop, your virtual file system, and the rest of your work space tidy avoids a chaotic mind.

Under-promise and over-deliver.

Buy yourself time with clients by stretching the timeline further than you think you'll need, and add a few hours on top of each quote or proposal for those small tasks. Then, when you come in under budget or before the deadline is looming, not only will your stress be minimized, but your clients will love you for it. This wise approach also gives you some much-needed breathing space, should anything go amiss.

Create routines.

The more routine you impose on your day, the quicker you complete the small tasks, because you aren't using the same brain power. It's the same feeling as driving along a road we travel constantly—as good as auto pilot.

Learn to say no.

Turning down a job is liberating, and can be very productive. If you're asked to pitch for a project for which you know you don't have the skills or time, or gives you a gut feeling that the prospect could become a difficult client, learn to trust your gut instinct and politely say no. This is far more productive than burning yourself out trying to undertake a project you should never have started, or lose money because you couldn't tackle the hours or timeline.

Manage your information.

Keep frequently referenced information nearby. Keep your email inbox organized, your file structure easy to understand, and physical files and materials in a logical order.

---

[4] http://www.rememberthemilk.com/

Turn off non-essential software notifications.

Those popup windows announcing you have a new email, or a colleague has opened their messenger just create distractions. Turn these off, and train yourself to check your emails and messages less often. Don't feel afraid to turn your email off completely for stretches of time; although often people expect email to be instant, there's really no need to respond within minutes when a few hours' difference won't hurt.

Plan your day.

Start by reviewing what needs to be done tomorrow before you finish for the day today, which allows you to have the day ahead stored in your subconscious. Then, first thing the next morning, do what you can to plan your day. Use a time sheet or similar tool to break your day into chunks, and assign tasks to each chunk. As you complete them, cross them out; this works as a good motivation tool.

Unsubscribe to infrequently read email mailing lists.

How many lists count you as a member, yet you never post to them or even read them? If you catch yourself deleting or marking as read weeks of mail list messages, it's time to unsubscribe.

Create templates for every document that you can.

There's no point writing a proposal or quote from scratch every single time. Develop a template that covers everything apart from the client name, project details, and costs. This same principle goes for a multitude of business documents. Invoices, account reminders, hosting renewals, service descriptions; the list goes on.

Work as hard at relaxing as working.

If you're working every waking moment of the day, I guarantee you aren't overly productive. Our bodies and minds need downtime as much as they need uptime. Make that relaxation time an important inclusion in your daily tasks.

Complete one task at a time.

Checking your email in the middle of a coding or design session can be disastrous for your effectiveness. Learn to completely focus on the task at hand before switching to the next.

Research and refine further improvements.

There are always new or different ways to approach just about anything in business, and this principle applies to productivity as well. Spend some time on a regular basis to have a look at what productivity ideas are out there, adopt the ones you resonate with, and then tweak them if required.

There are some great productivity blogs worth reading, such as the well-known Zenhabits,[5] 43Folders,[6] and aptly named Lifehack.[7]

Books I recommend picking up for further reading on this subject include David Allen's fantastic productivity bible, *Getting Things Done: The Art of Stress-Free Productivity*,[8] as well as the informative *Work Smarter, Not Harder* by Jack Collins and Michael Leboeuf.[9]

Organizing Your Tools

The constant progress in the world of software means that more and more applications that once were only installable are now downloadable.

This development has massive benefits for those on the move, and those who may use more than one computer for their work. Being able to use applications from all sorts of devices from anywhere on the planet makes a freelancer far more versatile and mobile.

Here are a handful of online applications you should consider when organizing your freelance setup.

Web-based email providers, such as Google's Gmail and YahooMail, offer unprecedented features, all for free. Many of these can be set up to work with your domain, which looks far more professional than a yourusername312@freewebemail.com address.

---

[5] http://www.zenhabits.net/

[6] http://www.43folders.com/

[7] http://www.lifehack.org/

[8] David Allen, *Getting Things Done: The Art of Stress-Free Productivity* (London: Piatkus Books, 2002).

[9] Jack Collins and Michael Leboeuf, *Work Smarter, Not Harder* (New York: Harper Business, 2000).

If you need those standard office-style packages, such as spreadsheets and word processing, you should take a look at web-based offerings; try:

- ZoHo (http://www.zoho.com/)
- Google Docs (http://docs.google.com/)

If you use multiple browsers on various computers, having your favorites in one place is fantastic. Two social book-marking sites well worth trialing are del.icio.us and ma.gnolia.

If you visit blogs and news sites, you'll find an RSS feed reader invaluable for keeping the news all in one place and boosting your productivity; check out:

- Google Reader (http://www.google.com/reader/)
- BlogLines (http://www.bloglines.com/)

Feeling lonely? Need to build your networks? Social networking sites, such as the mammoth Facebook and well-known professional-targeted LinkedIn, are great for building a freelance network, and making new friends.

Instant Messaging takes on a new meaning with applications such as Twitter, which transforms messaging from its traditionally one-to-one origins to a one-to-many basis. There's also the web-based Meebo, which allows you to use multiple instant messenger systems from one web page, all at the same time.

Established sources and newcomers to Customer Relationship Management (CRM) and Sales Software are also available online:

- SalesForce (http://www.salesforce.com/)
- Highrise (http://www.hirisehq.com/)
- Entellium (http://www.entellium.com/)

Need to receive the occasional fax, but don't need a machine sitting idle in the office corner? You may wish to investigate fax to email services, such as:

- MyFax (http://www.myfax.com/)
- utBox (http://www.utbox.net/)
- Popfax (http://www.popfax.com/)
- eFax (http://www.efax.com/)

Voice over IP (VOIP) is an exciting revolution in telephony, using the Internet as the delivery medium. See services such as Skype (http://www.skype.com/) and Net2Phone (http://www.net2phone.com/) to see how cheap calls can be; the downside is that there may be issues with voice quality. And do you need to access your main computer remotely? Check out services such as GoToMyPC (http://www.gotomypc.com/).

Registering Software

A common shortcut for many freelancers trying to save some money from that start-up costs drain is to skimp on licensing for software. This may seem like a cheap way to avoid a few hundred or thousand dollars in the short term; however, if you get caught, the fine will far outweigh any savings.

Software piracy doesn't even need to extend to downloading cracked copies of software from dubious web sites. Many licenses prohibit installation using the same license key on more than one computer at an one time, so be sure to read the license in detail before loading up the same suite on your desktop and laptop computers.

For more information on software piracy and why it hurts software manufacturers and possibly yourself, visit the Business Software Alliance web site.[10]

Don't forget that there are often free, open source, or very cheap alternatives for many software packages, which are a perfect stop-gap if the budget is tight, and perfect if you only need the package occasionally.

Backing Up Regularly

One of the most common—and potentially most serious—oversights on the part of many freelancers is the failure to back up their own and their clients' data *religiously*. Sure, you may lecture clients about the importance of backing up their data, but have you taken the time to create a method for your own backing up?

Check with your hosting company: does it back all of your clients' web sites up frequently? Whatever the answer, add extra precautions and create your own scheduled backups. Plan now rather than risk a failure that has the ability to kill your business and reputation.

---

[10] http://www.bsa.org/

In an ideal world, you'd back everything up every day and store it somewhere offsite. In reality, most freelancers baulk at that level of efficiency; however, it doesn't need to be so hard. Take a moment to look at your requirements. Most likely, you will have one hard drive storing all of your project and work files, and possibly another hard drive (or the same drive) containing all of your installed software.

Given your software inventory doesn't change all that frequently, you can start by ensuing that you have all of the original installation disks and any further updates or workspace tweaks burned to CD or DVD media. These can be stored either in your home or office, or ideally at another location, such as your parents' house or with a friend living nearby.

Then we have the meat of the data: your project files. These are the code libraries, design files, project documents, and email archives. The simplest method is to back up rarely changing files (such as your applications, settings, and so on) by occasionally burning the data to a DVD or CD, and to back up frequently used data using both online services *and* DVD or CDs for weekly or monthly backups. A common method is to back up your absolutely critical data, such as passwords, to a thumb drive or an external hard disk drive which you carry with you or store somewhere away from your normal work space.

There are many online solutions now for backups. Some offer free plans, and quality really varies between providers—be careful making a decision about hosting of your private data without first seeking reviews and obtaining advice. A few of the more popular online backup systems include:

- Mozy (http://www.mozy.com/)
- iDrive (http://www.idrive.com/)
- DriveHQ (http://www.drivehq.com/backup/)
- XDrive (http://www.xdrive.com/)

An ideal situation would involve having offsite storage through an online provider, and a local backup using other media such as an external hard drive. This way, if the online provider falls in a heap, or you lose your disks, there's a second source of recovery.

Consider investing in a local server for your home or office. This can be set up to take scheduled backups of all your local and online files.

Be sure to actually check backups frequently—and ensure you can restore data. It's pointless to back up to some form of media nobody has access to nowadays (for example, 5.25" floppies fall into this category!).

Polishing Your Contracts

Soon enough, you'll be asked for a written quotation. This is your chance to show your prospect how serious you are, by writing a great proposal and agreement document, and not scribbling a few numbers on a napkin!

You'll also probably discover you'll need some other contracts and documents fairly soon. There's a few great ways to start the process, firstly start by determining what documents you are likely to need. Common documents for freelancers are a Proposal or Quotation, a Contract, and perhaps a Non-Disclosure Agreement.

The good news is that most contracts and non-disclosure agreements are fairly standard the world over. You can pick up templates from anywhere (with permission, of course!), tune them to suit your requirements, and have a legal eagle pass an eye over the finer detail. There's even great business template software such as Business-In-A-Box,[11] free business document web sites such as DocStoc,[12] and don't forget Brendon Sinclair's invaluable *Web Design Business Kit 2.0*,[13] which features plenty of contract templates, not to mention a truckload of other great business reading.

Case Study

Emily

In her previous role at a large media company, Emily had to be super-organized to manage her daily routine. This experience has really given her an edge in making the transition to freelance, as she already had good time-management and productivity habits.

---

[11] http://www.biztree.com/
[12] http://www.docstoc.com/
[13] Brendon Sinclair, *The Web Design Business Kit 2.0* (Melbourne: SitePoint Publishing, 2007); http://www.sitepoint.com/kits/freelance2/

With the business structure all sorted, and a few small projects underway, Emily is aware that she needs to keep the momentum up and not slacken, just because she now has nobody to answer to.

At the same time, Emily doesn't want to get caught in the seven-day-a-week trap, which she has seen other freelancers fall into. Marking out weekends as her own, Emily hopes to contain her freelance hours to normal weekday business hours. She is working in the spare room of her flat, so it's doubly important she keeps work and leisure separate—she's already eyeing her favorite local cafe as an alternative work space for when she begins to feel isolated.

Emily is using her Outlook calendar to schedule her meetings and block out hours for projects. She's also using reminders each day for lunch and occasional breaks.

Jacob

Jacob has work to do in the productivity area; however, it is a huge positive that at least he's aware of it. Possessing a confident, outgoing personality, Jacob needs to work on putting in the planning before making rash decisions about how much to quote or what timeline he can meet.

Jacob is using an online accounting application, so he's chosen a web-based time tracking application that can tie in with his account-ing package. This way, Jacob can be very aware of the difference between quoted and actual hours, and work on his other development areas in the meantime.

Jacob's family has a large home, so he has marked off a room at the front as his office, and bought some great furniture from a disposals outlet. That, coupled with good natural light and some artwork on the walls, has given Jacob a comfortable but professional place to work.

Jacob has embraced as many web applications as possible as a way of keeping costs down, as well as allowing access to his calendar, accounts, backups, and other files from anywhere he might be.

Summary

First up in this chapter, we discussed a number of factors to consider when choosing the location of your home office. We also went into some detail about the basics of ergonomics and what to look for in a chair and desk.

We discovered the importance of keeping work and life separate, with some tips and hints on how to achieve this. It is extremely important for both yourself and those close to you that you do your best to have a great balance.

We then looked at the number-one tip for freelancers; tracking your own time. We also looked at the importance of scheduling, and went through some ideas and tips for improving your own personal productivity. There are some great online tools out there to help with productivity, and we went through some of these, as well as discussing contracts and the benefits of keeping all your software licensed.

We wrapped up by talking about that which we all hope to never rely on—backups. I'm sure you'll agree that any freelancer who doesn't back up their work is destined for disaster, and this is not a lesson best learned after such an event.

Now you're all set up and ready to go, we'll look at how to gain that all-important freelance work.

Chapter **5**

Win the Work

If there is one word that stops many fledgling web freelancers in their tracks, it's *selling*. The concept of being a salesperson is one that makes many designers and developers break into a cold sweat, when really, selling isn't the bogeyman that we often assume it to be.

If you can embrace the basics of sales, and become comfortable with the idea of self-promotion, you are so much more likely to become a success than if you don't. It's a sad fact that many freelancers never engage with this element of freelance life, and it's frequently a factor of them abandoning freelancing.

It doesn't have to be a subject of dread, though. In fact, it just *isn't*. Everyone sells and promotes themselves all the time; they just aren't often aware of it. When you apply for a bank loan, when you ask your boss for a raise, when you go on a first date—these are all basically exercises in selling and promoting yourself.

In this chapter, we'll start by talking sales: learning to sell, and understanding what you offer. We'll discuss what it is that your client base wants from you, and also put some thought into what constitutes the ideal client by creating a profile. Then we'll review your competitors, develop your Unique Selling Proposition, and look at the sales process.

We'll also discover that all-important sales funnel, look at methods to overcome the fear of selling, and consider the best way to ask for referrals.

Then you'll pick up some tips on how to brand yourself, look at ways to network both in real life and online, consider the place of social networks, and uncover other methods of self-promotion, such as public speaking, marketing and advertising, and creating your own blog.

We'll also hear from well-known public speaker and author, Molly Holzschlag, about the the key points of self-promotion.

Learning to Sell

This is the big one. Unless you can embrace the concept that selling is a vital part of your freelance endeavors, you will fight an uphill battle. Often, your selling ability will be the only way you can win a project rather than see it go to another supplier with similar skills.

Put aside that stereotype of a slick salesperson with a rapid-fire spiel, risibly over-familiar demeanor, and high-maintenance hair—there's no need to be anything you're not. The basis of your sales efforts are as simple as this: as a web freelancer, you sell solutions to customers' problems. If you can effectively and confidently communicate your solution, and convince the customer to go with you, you'll be the one building the solution as well.

Effective selling isn't as hard or complicated as many of the books and sales courses out there may lead you to believe. There are really only five requirements to be able to sell your own services:

You must have self-belief.
> If you don't have an absolute belief in your own abilities, you'll have trouble selling them. Since you're going freelance, it can be assumed you are already confident about your own abilities, and you need to allow that confidence to shine though everything you do and say.

Shake off that self-doubt monster, and be proud of your accomplishments. Learn to stand up and say you are great at what you do, and be ready to prove it.

You need to believe in the solution.

If you wouldn't use the proposed solution yourself, don't offer it. You need to trust your recommended solutions; understand that if you don't, it's likely to show in your body language and the way you approach the sale.

Consider everything you propose as though you were buying it yourself—what does the prospect really want to gain from the solution? Make sure you explain the benefits in an easy-to-understand way to your prospect.

If there's something you are unsure of, admit it. If you promise solutions you aren't confident in delivering, it'll come back to bite you.

You must learn to handle rejection.

Rejection is a bitter pill to swallow at first. You'll feel personally affronted when somebody says no the first few times, but you need to understand that its business, not personal. You need to develop a thick skin when it comes to rejections in sales—you won't win 100% of the work you pitch for.

Always remain gracious and courteous when being turned down. This is the most professional way to handle the situation, and keeps the door of communication open for possible future projects.

Salespeople often refer to sales as "a numbers game"—the more rejections you can endure, the closer you are gaining to an acceptance.

You need to be able to communicate effectively.

This is a very important skill to have in all facets of freelance life, most of all when the time comes to sell your services to your prospect. You need to be able to communicate your message and ideas effectively and ensure that the recipient understands them.

Remember that communication is not just verbal and written. Consider the art of active listening—do you really understand the prospect's problem? Take the time to listen, and reiterate what they are saying when appropriate so that they know you understand. Propose solutions to their problems; don't try to sell them a solution they may not need but is easy for you to sell. It's these little extra steps that can make a huge difference to your reception.

You need to try different techniques.

I've read over 20 books on sales and the art of selling in the last ten years. Not one of those books actually emphasizes the same thing. Sure, they touch on similar concepts, but the point proved by their differences is that selling really is a personal journey. Although there are some fantastic tips and concepts in all of those books, you need to have absolute confidence in yourself to use them. If you aren't, you'll come across as unsure. Try different techniques, read lots of books, blogs, and articles on the subject of selling, and find what is natural to you.

To start with, a few good places on the Web include Paul McCord's Sales and Sales Management Blog,[1] Eyes on Sales,[2] and the Sell Your Services section on SitePoint.[3]

If you read "a selling method" and cringe because you believe it sounds sleazy or won't work, don't try it—it's that self-belief rule. If you don't believe in the sales process, how will the prospect?

Selling is really a conversation. You discuss the problem, you suggest a solution, and the prospect either takes it or leaves it. If you can put a tick next to the five requirements above, you'll do well in those conversations.

Determining Your Offering

When you're a freelancer, there's a great temptation to attempt to be everything to everyone, and to be known as an expert in every area. You'll soon come to realize, however, that not only is this a very difficult act to achieve, but also it isn't what your clients actually want.

What clients want are experts in whatever service they currently seek. They don't want a "we do anything, anytime" (to borrow a phrase from *The Goodies*) person,

---

[1] http://salesandmanagementblog.com/
[2] http://www.eyesonsales.com/
[3] http://www.sitepoint.com/cat/sell-your-services/

who is average in many fields. They want someone who specializes in web design, web development, user testing, project management, or whatever it is you offer.

Become a Specialist

If you're naturally good at design, development, and just about everything in between, that's great. But you should concentrate on what you are very good at, and what makes the most money. Over time, you can refine your growing business from being broad to very specialized.

By evaluating your own skills matrix, listening to your existing clients, and understanding what your perfect client wants, you can develop a more finite services offering, which takes into account both what you are actually good at and what your clients actually want.

Don't hesitate to partner up with other freelancers with complementary skills; between the two or three of you, you can work as a team to deliver the project, sharing the resources and responsibilities.

Asking Prospects What They Want

Now, let's deal with the other side of establishing what it is you offer. Determining what your prospect wants sounds so simple and obvious, and it's hard to believe more people don't treat this as the starting point it is. The best way to gain an insight into the mindset of your customer base is to simply ask them. You can ask them one on one, at the start or close of a project (bribe them with a free coffee), or set up a simple web-based survey, asking key questions to help refine your offering.

This is a fantastic way to do some very cheap market research into a new product or service offering that you're considering as well. A simple survey with a few of questions followed up with an email of gratitude does two things. Firstly, it gives the recipient the feeling that their views and opinions are important to you; secondly, it gives you some fresh angles and ideas with very little effort or cost.

Two web-based survey services each offering a limited free plan are the very slick Survey Gizmo[4] and eSurveysPro.[5]

---

[4] http://www.surveygizmo.com/
[5] http://www.esurveyspro.com/

Creating an "Ideal Client" Profile

Creating a profile of what you consider to be an ideal client is a very interesting exercise, and can provide great insight as to what direction you should be taking in business. The run-on effect is that this process can help you become choosier about the prospects and clients you wish to deal with, as your business grows.

If you have existing clients, with any luck you can point to several of them and say, "They are my ideal client." An ideal client comprises:

- a client who wants your services
- a client who can pay for those services
- a client who will work well with you

Let's look at these three statements in some more detail.

A Client Who Wants Your Services

First, you want clients who actually want your services. You can spend extraordinary amounts of energy attempting to influence someone who doesn't believe in the Web that they need a web site, but at the end of the day, you're all too likely to be wasting your breath.

Let's define this further. Who actually wants your service? Well, not most of the population, I'm afraid. We can refine the question to apply to people or organizations that actually need web sites. Can we refine it further? Sure! It'd probably be safe to say small- to medium-sized businesses and organizations looking for a new web site.

You may want to refine this even more by focussing on those small- to medium-sized businesses within a certain geographic area, which could be your town, city, or even state. This won't rule out the occasional international project; however, it will help to bring some direction and concentration to your sales efforts.

A Client Who Can Pay for Those Services

Looking back at the rates we calculated in Chapter 3, who can afford you? It's fantastic to have a long list of prospects; however, if they can't pay, you can't eat. You'll need to qualify prospects, and ensure they can actually afford your services or product—and do this early on.

You can qualify a client's expectation of budget during the first meeting by asking if the company has a budget set aside for this work, or suggesting an average budget range and watching for a reaction, or even being up-front during the first phone call and stating something like, "My projects generally cost an average of $5,000," for example.

This approach potentially saves you and the prospect time, as it weeds out those who aren't prepared or are unable to pay professional rates before you've spent a lot of time working together to define the needs for your proposal.

Perhaps you've chosen a fairly healthy billable rate. In this instance, we may want to define the ideal client further now, as "not price conscious and happy to pay a premium price for quality."

A Client Who Will Work Well with You

Last in this equation is a harder expectation to define—clients who will work well with you. We all have those nightmare clients now and then—no matter what we do, they're never pleased and we'll never see eye to eye. It's times like these when you may be tempted to get out that jousting outfit; however, if we can simply avoid those types in the future, we'll all be happier.

Now, unless you have a crystal ball or psychic abilities, you won't be able to absolutely define clients who will be a dream to work with, but learn to trust that gut feeling you experience after the first meeting or two. If you have a feeling that a prospect is going to be more trouble than they're worth, consider strategies to avoid that project, some of which we'll discuss shortly.

When you consider any marketing activity, or indeed when you complete the sales process, compare your likely leads against this ideal client profile, and then do your best to win the ones that match closely to your ideal client.

Reviewing Your Competitors

Actually determining what your competitors are offering is an often-overlooked step in defining your own offering and researching what the market needs.

This task may sound difficult, but with a little time, it's usually fairly trivial to get an understanding of what your direct competitors offer. Start by defining your nearest competitors, and visit their web sites.

Look through the content and do your best to try to understand who they are targeting, and what services they offer. If you can, look at some of their folio of work to gain a better picture for the types of clients they work with.

If this tactic doesn't work through lack of information on their site, be cheeky and call or email them (use a pseudonym, obviously—this is where Gmail, Hotmail, and other web-based email services come in handy) and ask them what services they offer. If this sounds dodgy to you, you should realize that just about every larger business performs this trick regularly to obtain an understanding of their competitor space. Another way of collecting this information is to ask people you know who have previously engaged competitors to build their web sites for their feedback on the experience—they will probably be happy to share the proposal or the final costs with you.

Armed with this information, you can make better judgments on what your competitors are doing right and what they're not doing so well. These insights may allow you to see opportunities in the market to target. If anything, this knowledge should help you determine your Unique Selling Proposition.

Developing Your USP

A **Unique Selling Proposition** (USP) is a powerful way of describing your business in a few short sentences. The concept behind a USP is that it quickly ascertains what distinguishes you from your competitors.

You can start developing your USP by answering a few key questions:

- What is unique about you, compared to your direct competitors?
- Which of these differences are most important to your prospective clients?
- Which of these differences can be easily communicated to your prospects?
- Can these differences be used to build a great USP?

Say you have focused on the not-for-profit or charity market, and have extensive experience in building successful web sites for this sector. You could use that experience, and the fact you are a solo worker to your advantage; you could develop a USP that states something along the lines of:

> I build web sites for charitable organizations, utilizing my experience and knowledge in not-for-profit areas, coupled with my personalized service and attention to detail.

A USP will help to answer questions from your prospects, develop your own confidence in what you do, and help provide direction for you into the future. Remember, a good USP clearly explains what makes your services unique; it isn't meant to be a mission statement.

Understanding the Sales Process

Irrespective of what professional services you are selling, the process is more or less the same. Five distinct phases can be identified in the sales process, and these are:

- establish credentials
- uncover requirements
- explore options
- propose solution
- close

Reducing the sales process to its essentials like this may make the whole process seem very simple—and really, it is. You start by making contact with a "suspect"—sales-speak for someone who may want your services—which could be initiated by either side; then, you establish your credentials. This is the point where you define what you offer, relate your experience in the field, and the like.

Then, your suspect becomes a "prospect"—more sales-speak: this means they're now interested in your services or products—and you move into uncovering their requirements (listening is a *huge* part of this step, albeit an important element all the way through). They may have a brief already prepared, or you may need to laboriously pull the information out of them to form one.

Listen Hard!

Effective salespeople are very good at active listening. This is the ability to really understand what is being said, not just hear the words. Make sure you pay attention to exactly what the person speaking is saying, feel free to paraphrase their points back for agreement, and engage yourself—and don't interrupt.

At this stage, once you understand their requirements, run through the options available to the prospect and arrive at a point of offering to write a proposal or quotation. Don't be afraid to suggest to the prospect options they may have over-looked, or recommend they don't go with options they bring up—as long as you can back up with the reasons why. This shows you're interested in a longer-term relationship, and that you have the ability to *consult*, not just *do*. If they are still agreeable at this point, you have a very good chance of working for them.

The proposed solution stage is the final step of the process. You describe your ideas and concepts in a document, which is normally emailed or posted. For a larger project, you may also put together a presentation, where you'll discuss what you believe is the right course of action, and deliver the details of the costs, timeline, and other information.

This document or presentation may change and need to be reworked a few times, based on the prospect's feedback. Remember, also, that you shouldn't launch into too much detail about the technical specifications—even if you can predict that level of detail at this stage, it's likely to change before the project develops very far.

After this stage you arrive at the make-or-break moment. Your presentation is in the hands of the prospect, and it's now when they might become a client—or they might turn you down for another supplier or because they've made a different business decision. This is often the point where most freelancers become unstuck. They're too afraid of the sales bogeyman to consider calling and asking the prospect if they have any further questions, or if they've come to a decision. This stage is the follow-up, which typically happens anywhere from three to ten days after the pro-posal is delivered.

This is not the time to become frozen and wait by the phone for the prospect to call and transform into a client. Stay front-of-mind; you should call or email about once per week for the next few weeks to ask for a decision, until one is given to you.

Don't harass, and be careful to not sound aggressive—politely ask if there is anything else you can explain or information you can provide to help them make a decision, and when they expect this decision to be made.

Often, they may already have made the decision. If they do say yes, well done—you've got a new client.

If they say no, try to discover what the reason was. I find a phrase along the lines of "Thank you for considering me, I appreciate the opportunity to offer my services. If you don't mind, could I ask for any feedback you may have about my proposed solution?" Taking this approach to rejection can be a truly eye-opening experience for you. And remember: no matter what is said, don't get defensive, don't take it personally, and learn from the feedback for the benefit of your future sales contacts.

Overcoming Your Fear of Selling

It's quite common, as I mentioned at the start of this chapter, to have an irrational but very real fear of selling. However, you'll really need to do your best to overcome this fear if you want to excel as a freelancer.

The first step you'll need to take is to understand exactly what it is you're afraid of. Is it fear of rejection or failure? Are you afraid of being too pushy? Are you afraid you'll magically transform into that sleazy sales stereotype?

Once you know what actually gives you that reluctance to sell, you can start work to overcome it.

Remind yourself of your successes. It's easy in sales, especially if you end up doing any cold-calling, to feel as though the world is against you and you can't sell a thing. Keep a list of previous sales success handy so you can refer to it often, and consciously build your self-confidence and enthusiasm.

Break out into a sweat as you approach a prospect? Try a smile. Sounds crazy, I know, yet it really works—and is strangely infectious. Not only will you start to feel better about attending the meeting, it's also very likely your smile will rub off onto others, and they'll be more receptive to your pitch.

Start head-on, with the scary things. If you have a list of sales tasks ahead of you, and one you just know you'll do your best to avoid, choose that one to do first. Once tackled, you'll feel much better and less apprehensive about the rest of that list.

Anticipate common objections by having an answer prepared. If you end up against the same objections time after time, you'd better learn to confront them. The best way is to bring up these sticking points before the prospect has a chance to.

Practice! The more you handle sales inquiries, make cold calls, have meetings, and prepare proposals, the better and more confident you'll naturally become. The old adage that practice makes perfect really rings true when it comes to selling.

Your fear of selling is largely avoidable if you reduce the process down to the simple steps above. Try them out, keep up the practice, and before long selling will feel like second nature to you. It won't take long before you'll find yourself wondering what you were afraid of!

Controlling That Sales Funnel

The concept of the sales funnel is a great way to consider the sales process; it's rendered pictorially in Figure 5.1. Basically, it starts with lots of suspects at the top, filters down to prospects, and then reaches outcomes.

It can be hard to juggle every lead that's currently in the pipeline—unless you have a method of tracking them. There are a number of tracking methods available to you. The simplest way is to keep a spreadsheet showing the contact names, details, notes, and dates. This is fine for a start, but as you progress, you may want to consider using CRM (Customer Relationship Management) software.

There are many different CRM products out there, ranging from simple contact databases to fairly automated systems. These tools integrate with your email program and track all contacts with clients, as well as supporting mail-merge reminder letters and the like.

Figure 5.1. The standard "Sales Funnel"

Here are just a few of the best CRM resources:

SalesForce.com (http://www.salesforce.com/)
The long-running SalesForce.com would have to be the largest web-based system around. It claims to have over 41,000 customers, and is very sophisticated—and it offers a 30-day free trial.

SugarCRM (http://www.sugarcrm.com/)
A commercial open-source product, SugarCRM has hosted, installed, and open-source versions. It is known as a very good alternative to the SalesForce.com software.

Highrise (http://www.highrisehq.com/)
This CRM tool comes from the crowd at 37 Signals; it offers a free trial, and its account options start from US$24 per month.

Zoho CRM (http://crm.zoho.com/)
This new contender sports some impressive features and is totally free for the first three uses, which makes it perfect for the freelancer.

No matter what system you wind up using, you need to control that funnel. There are prospects to qualify (are they your ideal client?), emails and calls to be made, and proposals to be followed up. Set aside some time every day to make funnel-control a routine; the more this becomes habit, the greater your success.

Asking for Referrals

An often overlooked strategy for finding new leads is to speak to your current clients. Normally, it's as simple as asking your clients to write a short testimonial upon completion of projects—and while you think of it, do they have any contacts who might require your services?

This is a fantastic method for those of us who aren't natural salespeople, as a referral inquiry typically means the referrer already knows your background and services. This also reduces your sales time, as most of the work has been done for you.

You can even follow up existing clients later on, and let them know that you love referrals. Happy customers are always open to sharing their experiences with others if asked right.

Don't stop at clients, either—write down every friend and family member you can think of, and get in touch with them to inform them you are out on your own as a freelancer, and would appreciate their getting the word out.

Do contract work with other freelancers. Having people in the industry ready to refer you is fantastic—your fellow freelancers then have someone to suggest when a client asks about something in which you specialize.

Don't forget to thank anyone who refers a prospect to you, and let them know what the outcome was. I send a card and a bottle of wine as a way of thanking anyone who refers a prospect, irrespective of whether the lead became a client or not—it's the thought that counts. Besides, you want to encourage them to repeat the favor!

Creating "Brand You"

Regardless of age, regardless of position, regardless of the business we happen to be in, all of us need to understand the importance of branding. We are CEOs of our own companies: Me Inc. To be in business today, our most important job is to be head marketer for the brand called You.
—Tom Peters, *Fast Company Magazine*, Issue 10, August 1997

We all have a fair understanding of what we call business or corporate branding. But have you considered that in one sense we are all walking personal brands as well, and that this is espeically true for the solo worker?

We all build a personal brand every day through our actions, attitudes, and character, often without realizing it. As a freelancer, your business and personal brands are often intertwined, especially at the start. Being a freelancer gives you the freedom to promote your personal service, and therefore your personality.

You can build further on your personal brand using a number of methods. Some successful methods include public speaking, writing articles or blogging, attending networking functions, and using social networks. Any mechanism that encourages a positive promotion of "Brand YOU" should be considered a good thing. Keep in mind that self-promotion should use a softly-slowly approach, as aggressive self-promotion may be construed as overly egotistical, and can easily work against you.

The following pages are some of the popular self-promotion methods in more detail.

Polishing Your Web Site

One of the first places a prospect is going to look for examples of your work is, fairly predictably, your own web site. Make sure that you've given this important representative of you and your work the attention it deserves. Have a current portfolio of client work, as well as a skills matrix or list of services you provide.

For designers, the portfolio can be linked to live web sites, or screen grabs of work you've done. For developers, have a web application to point to, or release code and libraries. Case studies are also useful, allowing a description of the work involved, the outcomes achieved, and ideally a testimonial from the client.

Networking in Real Life

Networking is truly an art. The ability to move effortlessly around a room, speaking urbanely with different people, projecting an air of confidence and control, and leaving a positive impression is a skill revered by many in business. It comes naturally to the lucky few; the rest of us must do our best to emulate it.

Being able to network effectively in social situations allows you to meet more people, which increases the opportunities of finding people who need your services, or know other people who do.

The first most important element to realize about networking is that it shouldn't be forced, it shouldn't be pushy, and it certainly shouldn't be one-sided. If you set off to a business luncheon or sundowner with the objective of handing out 100 business cards, to dominate every discussion regardless of how glazed the eyes of your audience become, or to press the flesh with a minimum tally, it would be far better for you to stay at home.

Networking is a great opportunity to meet others, contribute to conversations, and to build your network, but it takes preparation and it involves perseverance.

You should first work on your introduction. This is a spiel of 10–30 seconds about who you are and what you do, often called an "elevator pitch." A good introduction clearly defines who you and your business, and invites further discussion.

For example, you might say, "Hello, I'm Emily Smith and I recently started a web design business, having worked in the industry for the last eight years." This introduction will encourage others to ask for further information.

 Name That Face

Do you have trouble remembering people's names? As soon as you've been introduced, repeat the person's name in your greeting, and again to any newcomers to your conversation as it progresses. The repetitive nature of this really helps nail the name into your memory.

The pre-event preparation consists of ensuring you dress appropriately and well, you have something to eat before you arrive (stuffing your mouth with food at every opportunity is not a good way to encourage conversation), and make sure you keep your alcohol intake to a minimum, unless you want to *be* the entertainment.

When you are at an event, start by finding people that you know, join their conversations, and introduce yourself to people whom you don't know in that group. As your confidence grows, you'll feel more at ease walking up, introducing yourself, and joining an existing conversation. Then, start stepping out of your comfort zone: approach people who look alone and strike up a conversation.

Take the time to ask lots of questions about the people with whom you're conversing, and make sure you are actively listening. Take heed of the well-worn maxim to avoid such subjects as religion or politics. Have a handful of questions at the ready, for when the conversation falters. Good questions include "How did you hear about this event?" "What do you have planned for the weekend?" and the like.

Encourage the exchange of business cards—you never know when someone may need your services, or know someone else who does. Be careful though; if you too obviously "work the floor" to hand out your cards, you'll quickly be seen as a charlatan—even when the occasion is specifically set up for networking. Be natural, participate in conversation, and offer your options; you'll seem like you know what you're talking about, and are genuine.

Alternatives to the Boring Business Card

Instead of boring business cards, especially if you're in a more creative line of work, think laterally and print postcards, stickers (such as Moo Stickers[6]), or even pin badges. This tactic will help you stand out from the crowd.

Join associations and networks in your area that can bring you prospects or may need something you can offer. Most of these associations have regular events, allowing you more networking opportunities.

Online Social Networks

There are a number of online social networks that have cropped up over the last few years, which can also be used to build professional and personal relationships.

---

[6] http://www.moo.com/

Two of the more popular ones used by professionals are LinkedIn[7] and Facebook.[8] LinkedIn is designed for professional networking, where Facebook is for a far broader audience. Both networking sites seem popular with business owners, though, so both are worth exploring—and both are free to join and easy to use.

If possible, use the same username on your various networks—your business name, if possible. This not only makes you easier to find, but helps to reinforce your brand. If the site allows avatars, use your logo or a good head-and-shoulders photograph.

LinkedIn and Facebook both have the facility to keyword-search people by name, location, and other fields. Another method is to upload a contacts list exported from your address book or email program, or allow access to your email software.

Online social networks offer a great way to build and forge stronger relationships with existing colleagues, and can be used as a method of virtually introducing others within your colleagues' networks. Join conversations, leave comments, and actively participate in as many ways as possible within these networks and on blogs and other web sites. Many people have reported excellent results in finding new recruits for their businesses, or meeting suppliers or business partners.

Be aware that there is a fair amount of netiquette around social networks, so it's a good idea to sit back and watch while you gain an understanding of the community.

---

[7] http://www.linkedin.com/
[8] http://www.facebook.com/

Public Speaking

According to most studies, people's number one fear is public speaking. Number two is death. Death is number two. Does that seem right? That means to the average person, if you have to go to a funeral, you're better off in the casket than doing the eulogy.
—Jerry Seinfeld

Public speaking is undoubtedly up there with the events people most fear. Yet it doesn't need to be. A little bit of research, some simple reminders, and much practice can make most people public-speaking superstars.

Don't worry about the nerves, they're a natural part of the exercise—in fact, it'd be a concern if you didn't have a little nervousness when standing in front of a group, as it may mean you're too complacent to give a great talk. Public speaking is a powerful method of making yourself known, and there are likely many opportunities within your local area to speak upon a topic of your choosing.

Many cities have groups and events that are targeted at small business owners—who are, more than likely, ideal clients for you. If you offer your knowledge by speaking at a local event, you have a good chance of practicing your public-speaking skills while making evident your knowledge, which may well wind up with you gaining a new client or two. You can start your search for a local association at web sites such as Small Business Administration[9] or SCORE.[10] Other ideal audiences can be found within many not-for-profit groups, such as Rotary International and Lions Clubs International.

A great book worth reading is the well-written *Presentation Zen*, the printed version of Garr Reynolds's very popular blog of the same name.[11] Garr talks about presentation design and delivery with plenty of full-color examples to keep you reading. Another good online source of public-speaking tips includes the aptly named Speaking Tips.[12]

---

[9] http://www.sba.gov/
[10] http://www.score.org/
[11] http://www.presentationzen.com/
[12] http://www.speaking-tips.com/

Marketing and Advertising

When we think of marketing and advertising, we normally conjure up the usual offline suspects of mass media channels, such as:

- television
- radio
- newspaper
- magazines
- billboards

However, these are mediums are rarely affordable for a freelancer, and they usually aren't targeted enough to be of much benefit. Do you really want to advertise your services to 15,000 insomniacs watching television at 2.00 a.m.?

These mediums do, however, present an opportunity for you to gain coverage by having a story or article written about you, your work, or your clients—clients may want to do a joint release with you, and they are guaranteed to love the benefits! This is where you'll need to understand how to write a press release, or find a PR consultant to do this for you. Many clients have their own PR people, so don't be afraid to suggest to a client that they should consider a press release. This may mean they'll do the hard work and you'll also get a mention.

Writing a press release isn't actually overly complicated, but it still needs to be newsworthy. I hate to break this to you, but an obscure technical subject that's tremendously exciting for you and your client may not be so interesting for a wider audience. Find some spin on the story that makes it exciting, especially if it can be fed to the mainstream and not just of interest to web developers. Then, corral some good quotes from stakeholders (your client, your client's customers, and yourself), and keep the whole release as succinct as possible—it really should fit onto one page.

There are plenty of places to find advice on writing excellent press releases, but here are the basics. A press release should open with "For Immediate Release," followed by a catchy headline, a slightly longer and more explanatory subheading (which may be used as an alternative headline), time and place, and then a few succinct paragraphs. Finish it up with "Press Release Ends" and make sure you include contact information for both yourself and your client, if it is related to a particular project. I've included a sample press release in this book's download file, which you can adapt for your own use.

Writing a great press release requires some skill with writing in a snappy, engaging manner; often, less is more. You may not feel that you have the skill set to write the best press release for yourself from scratch; if you know a PR person, offer to swap services with them for a mutual win–win, or consider one of the large press release distribution services, which can be very cost-effective. Try to grow more confident and adept at writing and distributing your own release, though; there are plenty of web sites and blogs that can provide advice and even feedback.

If all else fails, you can also approach these same media outlets, and ask if they need a "web expert" to write the occasional article for them. An offer of free or cheap content normally has editors pricking up their ears, and can result in more exposure for your business.

If there is a local business, or other publication that specifically targets your ideal clients, you should investigate their advertising options; however, be cautious about spending too much of your marketing budget until you see some results.

Look at advertising in your local phone book. It still surprises me how many people look in a telephone directory for a web company. In this day and age, it would be reasonable to assume that they'd search online, but it's surprising how many people out there still prefer to thumb through a phone book. Consider paying for a very small display advertisement, enough to have your URL, name, phone number, and perhaps a few dot points on what service you specialize in. Leave the big costly advertisements to your competitors, unless you can afford it and can see real benefit.

Another often-overlooked offline method is sending direct mail. Many businesses report good successes with these; however, be careful about who you target and where you obtain your lists from—out-of-date lists, or sending hundreds of letters to companies who are unlikely ever to use your services, is just a waste of time and money.

Consider sponsoring a local charity or event by constructing, updating, or maintaining its web site in exchange for sponsorship status. This not only helps a needy organization, it also puts your name out there. If you're going to sponsor a charity in kind, ensure that you both are clear about what the offer does and doesn't include, and make sure you get adequate sponsorship recognition for your hard work. You'll often notice many charity boards are largely populated by corporate businesspeople, who may just be your ideal clients.

To turn our attention to online marketing, now, we'll find plenty of methods you can engage with to see which works for you. First off, spend some time to gain an understanding of search engine optimization (SEO), if you don't know a lot about this subject already. SEO is an important element for most web companies, as those who aren't looking through phone books are likely searching on Google for you.

Here are some great resources to help keep you up with the latest in SEO:

- SEOMoz (http://www.seomoz.org/)
- SEO Chat Forums (http://forums.seochat.com/)
- SEO forum on SitePoint (http://www.sitepoint.com/forums/)
- SEO Book (http://www.seobook.com/)

Look at PPC (pay-per-click) advertising. Say, for example, you want to capture the attention of people in your state or country, searching for **web developer** on the major search engines. It's likely to cost a lot less than you think to trial a Google Adwords or Yahoo Search Marketing campaign for a month.

There are also other text advertising services, such as Text Link Ads,[13] which allow you to choose the web site or blog that your text advertisement will appear.

Blogging

Blogging is possibly one of the cheapest and easiest methods to get you out there and joining in the conversation. Armed with a domain name, hosting, a bit of time, and your choice of free blogging software such as Wordpress[14] or Movable Type,[15] you can join the 112.8 million active blogs (according to Technorati[16]) discussing everything and anything from freelancing, business, and web development techniques through to craft, personal opinions, and family reunions.

---

[13] http://www.text-link-ads.com/
[14] http://www.wordpress.org/
[15] http://www.movabletype.org/
[16] http://www.technorati.com/

Now 112,800,000 other blogs may seem like a lot of competition, but there's still plenty of opportunity to rise above the noise and be noticed. Blogs are essentially search engine- and user-friendly, due to blogs allowing multiple ways of sourcing information, the frequency of blog updating, and the engine room of blogging, RSS (Really Simple Syndication). RSS means that bloggers can have multiple ways of broadcasting their writing: everything from the traditional view-my-blog using a web browser to RSS feed readers and RSS via email, which means that you can get your blog fix on computers, PDAs, phones, media centers, and more.

Blogging can be powerful for not just personal branding, but also for the benefit of your freelance business. Over the last three years, my own blog has covered just about every subject I can think of. There's been a broad mixture of personal, business, and web industry news and articles, and even without much focus I've gained regular readers and even had new clients come on board as a result.

You could start by setting up a blog, and post articles on tips and tricks you've learned in starting freelancing. Alternatively, you could write about web development or design techniques that you've learned or discovered. Your blog could be about some of the recent projects you've worked on—ask permission of your clients, of course—or a way to express some of your wider creativity through writing and photography.

Some great places to start are by reading and commenting on other blogs. You can search for blogs that interest you via sites such as Technorati and Google Blog Search, and check out the blogroll on your favorite blogs. Find blogs with similar subjects to your own, and make a habit of commenting when appropriate. Use your blog URL if you can, to encourage people to visit your blog and interact across the blogosphere.

There's a plethora of blogs specifically concerned with blogging, too. Have a look at some of the recent posts at:

- BloggingTips.com (http://www.bloggingtips.com/)
- Lorelle on Wordpress (http://lorelle.wordpress.com/)
- The Blog Herald (http://www.blogherald.com/)
- ProBlogger (http://www.problogger.net/)

Funnily enough, there are some good books on the subject of blogging too. *Dispatches from Blogistan: A travel guide for the modern blogger* by Suzanne Stefanac,[17] as well as Chris Garrett and Darren Rowse's recent release, *ProBlogger: Secrets for Blogging Your Way to a Six Figure Income* are a good start to your collection.[18]

Remember that your blog should be professional in the style and the content; after all, it is a big advertisement for yourself. Also, avoid overly self-promoting—you may find readers leaving never to return. Be aware, too, that a good blog takes energy and time to establish and keep growing—it needs constant attention and regular posting to really flourish.

Writing Articles

There are plenty of web-based magazines, blogs, and web sites that publish articles, and there will be some of those who target your prospective client base.

Why not spend an afternoon or a few evenings writing an article on something in which you specialize, and submit it to a handful of places? Most web-based media allow unsolicited submissions, and although many don't pay, there's ample reward in the exposure to new prospects.

Don't forget to mention the article, once it has been published, to your existing clients—seeing their web professional writing articles for trade magazines or similar is an excellent reinforcement that they made a great decision to use your services.

Interview with Molly Holzschlag

Molly E. Holzschlag is a well-known web standards advocate, instructor, and author of over 30 books. She is Group Lead for the Web Standards Project (WaSP) and an invited expert to the HTML and GEO working groups at the World Wide Web Consortium (W3C).

---

[17] Suzanne Stefanac, *Dispatches from Blogistan: A travel guide for the modern blogger* (New Riders Press, 2006)

[18] Chris Garrett and Darren Rowse, *ProBlogger: Secrets for Blogging Your Way to a Six Figure Income* (Wiley Publishing: Indianapolis, 2008), http://probloggerbook.com/

Via each of these roles, Molly works to educate designers and developers on using web technologies in practical ways to create highly sustainable, maintainable, accessible, interactive, and beautiful web sites for the global community.

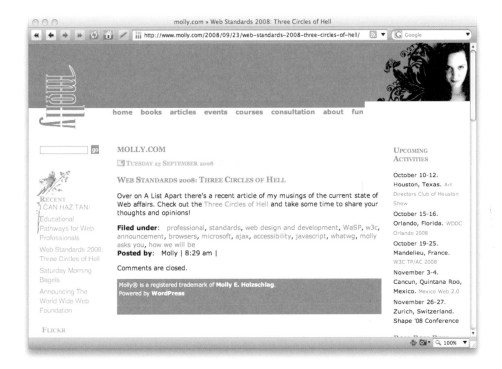

Figure 5.2. molly.com web site

I asked Molly a few questions around the topic of self-promotion:

When I think of personal branding in the web industry, you always come to my mind. You've developed a "personal brand" perhaps unwittingly; what do you attribute this to? Books, appearances, and your professional output with the projects you are involved with?

One thing that's helped me is having a short first name, "Molly," and the good advice and skills to nail the domain "molly.com" very early on. I don't think I'd have been as successful at having a name brand if I'd ended up with "holzschlag.com"! So that was a piece of the process which set up a solid future of personal branding on the Web.

I think the rest really came from the fact that I'm a social person and wanted to get out and meet people. So I'd say more than books, it's been meeting people, developing friendships and collegiate relationships that have bumped up the Molly brand into something meaningful.

When we talk networking, it's easy to suggest building up a network of contacts, but it's often harder to start off if you are relatively unknown. Do you have any tips on how to begin this journey of "getting out there"?

Meritocracy has been the foundation of getting ahead on the Web, and while that is changing over time with more demand for education, certification, and so on, we can use the tools we have to get out there, as you say. Social networks such as LinkedIn are fantastic for the professional, and there are so many social networks that people can take advantage of to build relationships via common likes and interests; you can't turn around these days without falling over one!

But clearly it takes commitment, having something interesting to say, and a willingness to keep at it over time. I've also noticed that people who are less outgoing struggle more with this, so there's a hurdle for those who are shy. Persistence and hunger pay off. To wrap up my thoughts on this, I'd suggest knowing what you want, and being persistent.

As someone who is obviously very busy in a professional capacity, as well as generating an enormous amount of output in terms of your writing, blogging, and conference involvement, how do you juggle this volume of work, and how do you prioritize your month?

I don't have any method. I'm very poor at organization, and I'm even worse if given some kind of organizational layer, such as productivity software. I function in complete chaos and it seems to mostly work for me, except for the occasional terrible oversight.

If you could give one tip to someone starting a career as a freelance web designer or developer, what would it be?

Know and be yourself. That may seem trite at first glance, but it isn't. Knowing yourself means you can determine your goals and how best to get them. For example, a person who does not embrace change and lifelong learning will not fare too well in this industry. Being yourself is what makes you interesting;

letting your natural character shine and your passion be evident is what gets people noticed!

Case Study

Emily

Emily has a select group of contacts which are bringing in some projects already. However, she knows she needs to build up this network if the projects are going to flow in. To this end, she has joined a few social networks. She has also approached a few small business groups in her area, offering to talk about the Web for small business, and already has a talk lined up.

On top of this, Emily has sent a letter with a handful of business cards to all her contacts, both professional and personal, and asked them to help spread the word that she's available for freelance work.

Although only three pages long, the proposal template Emily is using fits her purpose and is being well received by her leads.

Jacob

Jacob is a natural networker, and has a large group of contacts already in his address book. He's had a number of referrals already, and has started to send a bottle of wine each time to the person who sent the prospect to him.

Jacob feels he has all the sales talent he needs at the moment, but has bought a few books from a local bookshop on sales and marketing to help him refine his pitch.

He's bought a proposal template online, and has changed the parts he needs to make it more personal. He uses this alongside his trusty spreadsheet of leads and follow-up tasks.

Summary

Well, with any luck the dreaded specter of sales has been banished to some degree, and you now have some familiarity with the art of selling. As we've seen in this chapter, it's all about knowing what you have to sell, and having confidence in your ability to deliver it—and in communicating that confidence to your prospect.

A vital part of effective and well-targeted pitching is asking clients and prospects what they want—it's actually not as hard as it may seem. Related to this exercise is the value of formulating an ideal-client profile; this really helps you to focus on where you should be spending your energy. In the same vein, review your competition and define your own USP to ascertain what part of the market you service. Behind all your sales efforts should be a solid organizational layer—there are many ways to maintain control of the sales funnel and keep track of your leads.

In the second half of this chapter, we discussed the art of promotion. Building your own personal brand is great for business, and the various forms of networking can play a valuable component in getting your name out there in the wilderness. Public speaking, once you have the hang of it, is another great way to impart knowledge and get yourself promoted to your ideal clients. Writing for online and offline media will help raise your profile amongst your peers and target market, and don't overlook blogging.

Marketing and advertising can be an expensive mistake if you're not careful. Start small with targeted niche media and keep an eye on the costs and results.

We ended this chapter with a few questions and insightful answers from Molly Holzschlag on what self-promotion means to her, and how Molly has achieved such success in her personal branding.

Now that your promotional efforts are beginning to pay off and your proposals are being accepted, it's time to look at how to keep those clients happy!

6

Give Great Service

Coming together is a beginning. Keeping together is progress. Working together is success.
—Henry Ford

It's easy, especially when working simultaneously on a number of projects, to forget a crucial component of your freelance duties: giving great client service. In this chapter, we'll discuss ways to not only ensure a consistent level of high service, but also to keep the client up-to-date and happy with your progress.

We'll start by looking at the basics of providing client service. From here, we'll discuss the benefits of great service, and look at some valuable communication tips.

An important part of great service is having great project management; we'll discuss this next, and look at methods to avoid that project killer: scope creep.

We'll tackle the thorny subject of problems: problem clients, and the problems that emerge from making your own inevitable share of mistakes along the journey. We'll discuss issue resolution, learning from your mistakes, dealing with those problem clients, and knowing when (and how!) to fire those clients.

We'll continue by discussing ethics, and what we can do to be as ethical as we can, when dealing with others and ourselves. We'll chat about what ethics are, and why they're more than just about being honest.

As we work through this chapter, there are two points to keep in mind. Firstly, as many studies have shown, the number-one reason clients leave a professional services firm is because they don't feel as though they are receiving good service. Secondly, it's an undisputed fact that it is far easier and cheaper to retain an existing client than it is to attract a new one.

These two points should be more than enough to convince you of the importance of delivering fantastic client service.

Benefits of Great Service

Being a freelancer means that you have an opportunity to stand out from the pack by providing excellent client service. Great client service means that your clients are likely to be happier to leave you alone to do your work, thereby reducing the overheads of lots of client queries; plus, there's a good chance your existing clients will refer you to other potential clients.

Some clients actually choose freelancers over larger firms because of the individual attention they expect to receive. Having the same person in the initial meeting, answering the telephone and responding to emails, and then actually doing the work is a great benefit; you should sell this as a point of difference to prospective clients.

Some clients, however, will be concerned that you operate a business solo. If they bring this up as a reservation or objection, you can reassure them by providing backup plans in case you fall sick and suchlike—informing clients that you have a pool of talent available to you is a great way to give them confidence. To this end, find freelancers with similar skill sets, whom you can trust. Having a reciprocal arrangement in case of an emergency is a great weight off everyone's shoulders.

Giving great service isn't as hard as you'd expect. Once it becomes a habit, it's an easy process. Always look for ways of bettering previous service bests; this will encourage you to exceed client expectations regularly, and benefit both your client and you.

An excellent book on this subject is Scott McKain's *What Customers Really Want*.[1] McKain suggests that there's a gap—represented in his book as six disconnections—between what most organizations offer, and what customers actually want. His basic argument is that we're too focused on using the right buzz-words, such as "customer service," instead of really working on the relationships we have with our clients—who, after all, are people just like you and me.

At the end of the day, freelancers have the opportunity to make customer service far more personal than a large firm ever could. Learn to use this opportunity to your advantage.

Basics of Client Service

Providing great client service can give you a massive edge over your competitors. Not only is it just plain good manners, giving great service also means that you'll have a client base that will refer you to others, be less likely to leave, and become real champions of your cause.

Great client service goes way beyond that practiced smile or the automatic "good morning" response when you answer the phone—it's a far more holistic approach to just about everything you do.

Great client service consists of these five elements:

- manage client expectations
- maintain high availability
- practice courtesy and respect
- practice honesty in all communications
- be proactive in your service

Let's discuss these elements now, in more detail.

Manage Client Expectations

Fom that first sales meeting, it is important to manage your clients' expectations if you wish to build a really worthwhile long-term relationship. Be open and up-front

---

[1] Scott McKain, *What Customers Really Want* (Thomas Nelson, 2005); http://www.scottmckain.com/

about your availability, the processes you follow, your rates, and what you believe the client's obligations to be.

The absolute golden rule here is that you should never make any promise unless you are absolutely confident of keeping that promise. Ideally, you'd be better to under-promise and over-deliver. For example, exaggerate the timeline and keep tight control on the deliverables—and then surprise the client by completing the work sooner and delivering more than the client originally expected. This system also gives you important spare time and budget up your sleeve, should something go wrong during the work. If anything, having that extra time and budget allows you to give your work that extra little polish.

Managing client expectations often comes down to having consistent processes and good project management principles. You and the client should both strive towards having a situation where there are no unpleasant surprises and everything remains under control.

Maintain High Availability

It is important, as well as courteous, to answer your telephone, return calls, and reply to your emails in a timely manner. When speaking with or emailing a client, you should create the impression that they are the only customer of yours in the entire world. This also means that you should never blame other clients or projects for missing a deadline or not answering a call; it almost always sounds like a lame excuse.

This rule needs some degree of balance, though—you don't want to become a slave to your email, and it's a common trap that can quickly become time-consuming and counter-productive. Given that 95% of emails don't need an answer within four or more hours, set some breaks between checking your email; otherwise, you'll never get the work done.

You should also ensure that your responsiveness is not taken as an open invitation to your clients to start calling any time, day or night. As we discussed in Chapter 4, it's important as a business owner that you manage your time, being acutely aware of that all-important work–life balance. You shouldn't have any guilt or doubts about switching your business line to an answering machine or voicemail in the evenings; it's an effective tool to combat those after-hours calls, and helps solidify your professional status in the eyes of your clients. Make sure you include your business hours and email address on your voicemail message. This approach provides a subtle hint to clients that emails are often better, and your business hours should be considered as reasonably fixed.

If you do answer the phone after hours, and it does turn out to be a non-urgent matter, you might consider delivering a subtle hint; explain that you are "out for dinner," or even "out with the family," and currently not near a computer. This polite hint should normally be clear enough for you to be able to follow it up with the stated intention to deal with the task tomorrow, and allows you to close with, "Would you mind sending an email to confirm?" This rule also applies for responding to emails—read them of an evening or weekend, if you must, but don't respond unless absolutely necessary out of normal hours. If you do, you run the risk of training your clients to believe that you are available at any time.

Obviously, if you are in a situation where there is potential for client emergencies (for example, the web site goes down and orders are lost), ensure that you clearly define what constitutes an emergency, state what the response processes are, detail any costs or contractual arrangements in writing, and make sure the client understands. You might use a cell phone or voicemail as point of contact for this purpose—ensure that you check these regularly over weekends and holidays to ensure you're up-to-date. There's nothing more frustrating to a client than an urgent call being ignored when a seriously urgent situation rears its ugly head: Server down! Web site hacked!

You might consider offering a reasonable loading fee for any work done after hours; this could be 30–70% on top of your usual rate. This charge is normally enough to scare away clients with trivial requests—their money is suddenly more important than you doing the work right now, this evening.

Practice Courtesy and Respect

Think of those times in your life where you've felt that you haven't received the courtesy or respect you've expected in that situation, and contemplate the reasons for why you've felt that way.

It may have been in a retail environment, or it may have been in an old workplace. We all have stories of feeling that we weren't attended to at a level we were happy with or considered appropriate. Maybe the person dealing with you was unattentive, dismissive, or came across as just plain rude. There are many lessons to be learned there; the first is to ensure that *you* always provide the courtesy, respect, and excellent customer service that you'd want to receive if you were in the recipient's shoes.

Never belittle a request, or speak of a client in a derogatory manner, irrespective of whether they are present or not. I've been in many situations where someone has complained about another person to me, and my immediate thought is, "I wonder if they say the same about me?" That, coupled with the risk that your rant or complaint may find its way back to your client, should be a good reason to always steer away from this situation. Furthermore, I've seen emails that complain about a client being accidentally forwarded to that client in an email thread—what a nightmare. Never, ever write something about a client in an email that you wouldn't be happy for them to read; it's just not worth the risk!

Be Honest in All Communication

Be honest, always. This is actually quite a challenge at times, especially in a situation where you disagree with a client. The practice of honesty, though, has some great results. You'll find that people will admire you for being open, and they'll be much more likely to reciprocate this honesty when you deal with them.

As an example, if a client of yours asks you about something of which you have little or no knowledge, let them know that you'll read up on it, or ask others about it, and get back to them. This is a fantastic double advantage—not only are you being honest, you're also offering great service!

Many people see honesty as the most important personality trait; as a professional, I don't believe there's any alternative to it. If you're caught out in a lie—no matter how small—your relationship with that client will be in tatters, and very hard to recover.

Save yourself from that situation by always being honest, and avoid having your ethics brought into question.

Be Proactive in Your Service

Consider all the instances you can remember where you felt as though you received outstanding service. If you're anything like me, it will be those moments where there were the little things. This may have been an extra-friendly welcome at your local cafe, or a super-fast turnaround to a technical support request. When you consciously think about it, it probably involved no extra work from the person serving you.

Be on the lookout for ways to go that extra distance. These can be deceptively small things, such as posting out a hand-written thank-you card at the end of a project, or bringing takeaway coffees for yourself and your client when visiting their office. Try sending a thank-you card to your client at a set anniversary after the project, say after three or six months. This is a nice way of letting the client know that you haven't forgotten them, as well as issuing a subtle reminder you're available, if they have future work.

Buying your long-term clients lunch once in a while is a great way to say thank you—as well as providing an enjoyable and legitimate reason for leaving the house. Take a few minutes before the occasion to check out the movements of the client's competitors, and their new systems or techniques, and make sure you let your clients know about it—they'll be pleased that you've taken some initiative to help their business, and are likely to ask you to implement a similar system for them. These lunches may seem to be merely good fun, but take the opportunity they provide to subtly up-sell your services, and attract new work!

Communication Tips

In this age of cell phones, BlackBerry emails, and instant communication, it's easy to fall into bad habits when it comes to responding to calls and emails. What stands out in my mind, when it comes to excellent service, are those calls and emails where the recipient made me feel that my call or email was super-important to them.

When answering the phone, ensure you say your business name first, followed by your name—studies have shown that callers have a better chance of recalling a person's name if it is announced after the company name.

Make time to focus on the call. If you try to talk on the phone, while rearranging your inbox or worse, continue to code or polish a design, it'll be evident in your voice. You'll sound uninterested and give the impression that the call has interrupted you. This may well be true, but obviously it's good practice to hide that fact.

If the call really is an interruption of a client meeting or making a looming deadline, let the client know you are currently tied up with something urgent, and that you can call them back in one hour or another defined time. We've all been deep into coding or designing, and disliked the interruption to our concentration—as long as you define a time to call back, and follow it up, your caller generally won't mind. Then, make sure you *do* call back!

Let them know when you'll be back in touch. Your speed of reply to telephone calls and emails can be directly correlated to increased sales and customer satisfaction. Prompt is profitable!

Have a well-scripted answering message on your machine or voicemail when you can't answer the call—and make sure it states your normal business hours and reassures that you'll call back as soon as possible. Investigate having calls diverted to voicemail when your line is engaged—this saves having to have two phone lines when it's only you answering the calls.

When calling someone, announce who you are and where you are from when the person answers—this saves time, and avoids the office people having to ask. A phrase like "Hello, it's Miles Burke from Bam Creative here; I was hoping to speak to Jenny Smith," is both polite and shows that you're confident—and is a habit worth forming.

Emails are often a cause of misunderstandings, especially with relatively un-savvy users. It's easy to cause offense or be misunderstood, so it's worthwhile ensuring you keep the tone light, and emphasize the friendliness. What you write can usually be interpreted a number of ways, and is dependant on factors such as the recipient's mood. It's a great habit to reread your emails before sending, and make sure they come across as friendly.

However, this is not an excuse to sound all buddy-buddy. It's more professional to end an email with "Warm Regards" or "Sincerely" than "Cheers" or other more casual tones. A more casual mode of address may come later, when you know your client well and your relationship allows for such familiarity; even then, though, allow them to lead the way towards a casual approach.

If you receive an email that has a worrying tone, call the sender. Quite often, what sounds terse in an email is actually friendly—you may be just misinterpreting it. If you do find an unmistakeably angry email in your inbox, resist the urge to send a hot-headed reply immediately, and take time to cool down. You'll find those deep breaths and time to analyze the contents can avoid misunderstandings and damaged relationships more than if you fire a response back straight away.

 Auto Answers

> Don't forget to set an out-of-office responder in your email, if you are taking a day or more off. This is worthwhile for sick days as well as holidays, and if out of town on business, when you know your connection could be flaky. Make sure it says when you expect to be back, and what to do in case of anything absolutely urgent (and word it that way too, to discourage non-urgent calls).

Always ensure you have a reasonably succinct email signature at the bottom of all of your emails, too—these are a fantastic way of reminding people of your URL and other contact details. If you regularly use your cell phone to send emails, consider adding "Sent from cell phone" as a signature. This indicates that you're mobile, and may not be able to respond to subsequent emails straight away. It also explains why your email was probably short, and helps excuse strange characters, spelling, and other weirdnesses thanks to predictive text software.

For more great email etiquette tips, have a look at Email Etiquette by Daily Writing Tips[2] and the infamous Netiquette Guidelines RFC.[3]

Project Management

Great service often boils down to ensuring consistent good service. By following a clearly defined process, built around good project management principles, you can take much of the guesswork out of a project and ensure that there is ample opportunity for any corrections that need to be made.

Over the last 15 years or so, from the vantage point of a number of roles within the web industry, I've found that the one recurring issue raised in customer service discussions is a perceived lack of clear communication or process explanation to the client.

---

[2] http://www.dailywritingtips.com/email-etiquette/
[3] http://www.ietf.org/rfc/rfc1855.txt

Clients may give the impression that they understand more than they actually do, so avoid overly technical talk. Keep everything in layman's terms, without being patronizing, and watch for glazed-look cues that you're confusing them with jargon. If you do confuse them, avoid speaking down to them; instead, use phrases such as "As you may know …" and "You probably already know this, but …" to allow you an opportunity to explain things in simpler terms.

Lack of understanding about processes is easily avoidable. Ensure you provide your client with a clearly written process document at the start of a project, and contact them regularly, especially at every major milestone, to keep them up-to-date with your progress. Even if there has been little progress so far, make contact to let the client know—they'll feel far more in control and involved than if there's silence from your end. This one rule will avoid many of the issues we can have with complaints or unhappy clients.

If you can, break the project down into many smaller chunks of work, or milestones, and let the client know as you complete each stage—this communication means that they receive more assurance that the project is still moving, and also helps to avoid scope creep, which we'll discuss in a moment.

For more information on good project management principles for the Web, make sure you read Meri Williams's excellent book, *The Principles of Project Management*.[4] Another great book is Kelly Goto and Emily Cotler's well-known *Web Re-Design 2.0: Workflow That Works*.[5] Online resources that I read include:

- A List Apart
  (http://www.alistapart.com/topics/process/projectmanagementworkflow/)
- Joel on Software (http://www.joelonsoftware.com/)
- 43 Folders (http://www.43folders.com/)

---

[4] Meri Williams, *The Principles of Project Management* (SitePoint Publishing, 2007), http://www.sitepoint.com/books/project1/

[5] Kelly Goto and Emily Cotler, *Web ReDesign 2.0: Workflow That Works* (New Riders Press, 2004) http://www.web-redesign.com/

Tackling Scope Creep

A large cause of angst between clients and freelancers is that of one party believing the other has unfair demands. In fact, much of the time it often boils down to a project suffering from that project-killer, **scope creep**.

Scope creep happens when extra functionality or items are added into the project that weren't part of the original specification. It most often occurs because the project wasn't clearly documented or defined at the start, or was just poorly managed during the project's lifetime. Scope creep is often the first sign that a project is going to end up causing trouble, and you need to nip it in the bud quickly.

Clients changing their minds, or trying to add more work to a project and avoid paying for it, is a feature of scope creep. It's important for both parties that you tame that scope creep monster quickly—leaving it to grow and envelop the project will mean that both parties will end up in disagreement. The client will feel your resentment as the budget and timeline blows out, while you'll feel pressure to get the work done quickly and may end up reducing the quality of your work as a result.

Ensure that you have a clearly defined brief from the moment the work is quoted. This brief often needs to be co-written by you and the client, and should basically list all of the works in as much detail as possible, along with an understanding of milestones, dates, and exactly what each party is obliged to do and provide.

Break down the work into large and then smaller steps. Ensure that the client is aware of these, and is also aware of what change process you may have (make it known that you favor a simple change request form, for instance—a sample Change Request Form, which you can modify and use, is available for download from this book's web site).[6] By sticking to these processes, you and your client will retain a clear understanding of the costs in terms of time and money of the scope changes.

---

[6] http://www.sitepoint.com/books/freelancing1/

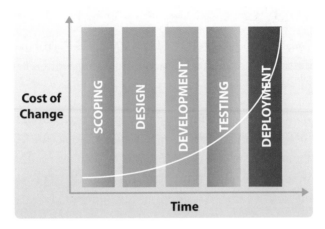

Figure 6.1. Cost-of-change diagram

The graph in Figure 6.1 provides a good way to illustrate to a client the impact of a change to the design or functionality of a web site at various stages of the project, and the cost of that change. Encourage all decisions to be made at the start of the project, preferably not in its middle stages, and *certainly* not just prior to its launch!

After each phone call or meeting that has included decisions about the deliverables, make it a habit to send a follow-up email outlining the decisions and any changes. This gives you a nice written record, the client will be grateful for the correspondence, and it creates evidence should the changes be questioned later.

Control scope creep by tying in any new requests to change requests, and outline the budget and timeline impacts of each change. Ensure that you clearly communicate when something is beyond the project's scope, and that you'll need to quote on it. You'll find that often clients will respond with, "Don't worry, it wasn't that important," to avoid paying extra.

Resolving Issues with Problem Clients

As much as we all like to believe it'll never happen, the truth is that clients complain and stressful situations do occur.

First of all, before we get to the genuine problem clients, let's look at the thorny issue of customer complaints. When a client complains about something you've done or your work, they are really giving you a golden opportunity. It may sound strange, but a complaining client may be a great client.

How so? Well, they're likely to be honest about how they feel, and if you can look past all of the emotion, and consider their criticism not as personal attack but constructive help, you'll benefit greatly from the experience.

I'd rather have a client speak to me about an issue, than to their colleagues. In this situation I have the right of response, but in the latter, I won't even know its happening. A client complaining to others is the reverse of being recommended, and something you want to avoid at all costs.

I've found quite often that complaints are normally driven by miscommunications or assumptions, both of which can normally be defused by giving a clear explanation and your commitment to sorting out the issue as a matter of priority. Don't let your ego get in the way—accepting blame, even when it may not actually be your fault, is a great way to defuse a situation and work towards a resolution. Starting an argument over who's to blame is a sure-fire way of exacerbating the situation.

However, as service-based workers, at one time or another we'll end up dealing with individuals, who, for want of a better term, we'll call "problem clients."

Rather than unpacking the jousting equipment beloved of our freelancing forebears, we can use some simple tactics to control the most difficult clients and situations.

Here are some techniques that I use when dealing with a client who may have unrealistic expectations, or is just plain difficult. Of course, these are good techniques to have at any time, with any client—difficult or not.

Discuss the situation, *not* the person.

> Let's not make it personal here. The situation your client and yourself are facing is to blame, not the stakeholders. Pointing fingers and looking for a scapegoat doesn't help either party head towards a resolution. Your client may be pointing the finger directly at you. Don't stoop to that behavior; prove to yourself and those around you that you don't allow a dispute to become a "blame game."

> And don't forget that it looks extremely unprofessional to blame a third party. Avoid pointing the finger at "the hosting company" or "your previous web developer" at all costs.

Consider your client's perspective.

Do your best to view the situation from your client's perspective. It can often turn out that, with a little empathy, you discover the true cause of your client's dissatisfaction, and you find clarity in resolving the situation.

You'll find it surprising that, quite often, it transpires that the root cause of the situation is something trivial, and that you'll be pleased to fix it.

I find much of this comes from an assumption on our part that a client understands the way something will look or work. Ensuring you always do your best to explain everything clearly normally avoids these situations.

Learn from your mistakes.

Your most unhappy customers are your greatest source of learning.
—Bill Gates

We all make mistakes. We need to admit them and learn from them. The best strategy here is to consistently have clear and open communication with your clients, at all times.

If you come across a situation that you've helped cause, own up to it early, and rectify it immediately. The longer you leave this situation, the more chance that the client will find out first and the more stressed you'll become before you admit to the problem.

Most clients understand that we're all human—heck, even they are! Just about any situation can be easily defused by calling the client and letting them know you've realized you've made a mistake, and you're very keen to fix it—let them know a time and an outcome to expect, and above all, make sure you stick to your promise!

Treat all clients with patience and respect.

When a situation starts to ignite, it can be an easy route to start interrupting and speaking over the other person. Whatever you do, avoid this behavior. It displays a lack of respect and will just fan the fire.

Show ras much respect and patience as possible, even in the most difficult situations. This shows that you are confident and always courteous, which often diffuses tension.

Avoid anger.

If you feel you are unable to stay calm, you should quickly terminate the meeting or call until you know you can respond and interact less emotionally.

If your client can't contain their anger, and starts to become abusive in any way, politely point out that you feel that their behavior isn't helping, and walk away or end the call politely and quickly—perhaps use a phrase like, "Let's continue this discussion when we've all calmed down."

Once you've had adequate time to soften those emotions, get in contact as soon as possible and get working on resolving the situation.

Be honest and fair.

You should always remain honest and fair. Don't be afraid to accept responsibility for anything clearly your fault—this shows a humility and eagerness to please, which is a pleasant surprise for most people.

This works both ways too—if you are being unfairly judged on something totally out of your control, don't hold back from saying so; however, be very aware of how you say it, aiming for diplomacy at all times.

Your goal is not to win an argument, but come to an agreement. Don't let your ego or competitiveness become a reason for a breakdown in a client relationship or project.

When All Else Fails

Sometimes you'll be faced with a difficult client situation that eventually becomes untenable. You should accept that not all relationships are worth saving, and that perhaps it's time to walk away from a project or client, if you can see that no resolution is possible. It may seem crazy to let go of a paying customer, but sometimes it can be the only way forward for both parties.

Rather than be unprofessional, retire the client carefully. You should always keep the situation civil. There are a few methods to firing a client gently:

- Let the client know that you've got enough projects on your plate, and that you can no longer handle their work.

- You can raise your prices substantially—this will either have the consequence of the client leaving you, or their paying you enough so that you no longer feel that they're such a problem.

- Just inform them that you've decided you can no longer meet their requirements. Keep it succinct and don't add any further detail.

In any of these outcomes, it's a nice touch to have a few names and numbers of people you can suggest who may be able to do future work for them—however, be wary of inflicting a true client from hell onto one of your fellow freelancers!

Being Ethical

The foundation stones for a balanced success are honesty, character, integrity, faith, love, and loyalty.
—Zig Ziglar

The importance of ethics in business simply cannot be overstated. In these times, it is certainly becoming commonplace to expect your suppliers and clients to have ethical business processes and actions, with an emphasis on non-economic values as well.

The same goes for you, and your business. No matter how large or how small, we all have a place in the community, and we all impact other people and businesses. As a freelancer, how you go about your business shows what sort of person you are to everyone around you.

Do you wear your trustworthiness on your sleeve? You should—people prefer to do business with others who are honest, open, and trustworthy. Start by being honest with yourself; understand your own strengths and weaknesses, your own likes and dislikes. When meeting with your prospects, clients, suppliers, or partners, always ensure you are sincere and genuine in your dealings. This includes being upfront and honest about your qualifications, expertise, and ability in projects being offered to you.

An ethical freelancer can be trusted to be honest and open in all of their dealings, ensuring that their reputation is built on trust, not false promises or making it up as you go. A successful ethical freelancer will not agree to take on work for which they are not suited. Turning down work can end up paying bigger dividends, if the prospect tells others how honest you were about your skills and the work being offered. I've had cases where I've turned down a project, and ended up with a larger project six months later as a direct result.

Trusted Recommendations

It's great if you can refer the prospect to someone else who can do the work; just be certain you can trust this other party to carry out the work to your standards. If they do let down your prospect, you'll end up looking bad as well!

An ethical freelancer will always treat everyone, including their competitors, with fairness and respect. There's no benefit to be gained by being underhanded with your competitors, or speaking negatively about them to your prospect or others. It makes you look bad to the person you're speaking to; if you do this to them, why would they not do this to you?

Ethics aren't something you tick on a form or mention in your quotes or proposals—running your business (and living!) ethically is something you need to consider regularly, and look for ways of improving your commercial impact on the community. This point is intentionally vague, and implies everything from being honest and trustworthy in dealings with people through to donating your services and even money to charities, as well as treating everyone around you in a way that you would like to be treated—with respect, dignity, care, and honesty.

Case Study

Emily

It's been a while now, and Emily has grown a nice stable of clients, most of which are actually web designers or small web companies that sometimes have overflow work. Emily is finding that, although they are a pretty relaxed bunch, they can be hard to handle at times. This chapter has helped Emily get on top of her project management, which is something she didn't previously consider as a client service issue, especially when dealing with other web people.

Although not overly advanced, Emily has started to include a very basic, one-page functionality spec with her quotes. Then, each time something changes, she updates this page and sends it back to her client so they're both on the same wavelength.

As for using the phone, since she's finding that cafes and client offices are becoming a frequent part of her working day, Emily has started to divert her office number at home to her cell phone when out of the office.

Emily finds herself fairly nervous broaching the subject of scope creep and asking for more money when the hours blow out. Having lost money on a few jobs, Emily is now quoting higher at the start, to avoid these situations, and has recently tried out the change request method, using the technical specs as a way of explaining the changes.

Jacob

Jacob is a natural talker, so finds it easy to embrace customer service. Having said that, he is aware of over-promising on a few recent jobs, and is aware of where he went wrong.

He is now exaggerating the timeline by a week or two on every job, which means that he can shuffle work around and still come in within time. This approach has fixed an issue of having disgruntled clients, a situation Jacob has encountered more than once over the last few months, due to his missing agreed deadlines.

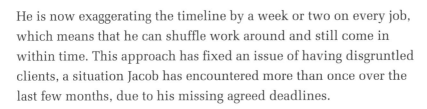

Jacob's biggest issue has been getting to grips with tracking his time effectively. He knows he needs to do it, in order to be able to quote better in the future; he wasn't doing it well when he first started out. He is now tracking his time using an online tool, and finding that when he is out of wireless coverage, a quick entry in a notebook suffices. This has shown him that he has under-quoted some aspects of his work previously, and he's quickly catching up with new projects as a result.

An issue Jacob is still working through is his inability to keep everything as strictly business—he keeps taking every criticism personally, and tends to react badly to this. With this in mind, Jacob has made a promise to himself to do his best to stay calm and take a moment of thought before responding.

Summary

Client service is paramount to your success. Just because you are the best designer or developer in the world, you're not excused from having to concentrate on providing excellent service—otherwise, your clients will walk. With some thought, we can provide excellent client service all the time. You've polished your coding or design skills—make sure they also have great "packaging," being your focus on excellent customer service!

We started this chapter with an overview of the basics of client service. I talked about the five cornerstones of great service, being:

- manage client expectations
- maintain high availability
- practice courtesy and respect
- honesty in all communications
- be proactive in your service

Then we discussed the benefits of great service, and looked at some communication tips when using the phone or email.

We looked briefly at project management, especially in dealing with scope creep, which is the cause of many disputes. We also looked at ways of resolving issues, and then discussed how to learn from (and admit to!) our mistakes.

Tackling problem clients is an important skill, and we discussed a number of strategies to keep them from becoming a problem. Finally, when all else fails, and the situation or client is untenable, we looked at ways to fire that client.

We also spoke about ethics, and leading an honest and ethical business life, and how important that is to everyone around us, as well as ourselves. It may sound corny, but it really is so true.

The two main points to remember? It's cheaper to keep an existing client than find a new one. And the main reason clients leave is because they believed they weren't getting great service.

Having discussed looking after our clients, in the next chapter we are going to discuss looking after *you*.

Chapter 7

Achieve Work–Life Balance

Looking after yourself goes beyond the concept of maintaining your physical health; it's a much more holistic approach, and it ensures your long-term well-being. As a freelancer, it's all too easy to overlook your work–life balance and emotional health, not to mention neglect the possibilities of supporting the wider community and looking after the environment.

This chapter will expand on that all-important work–life balance I've mentioned before, looking at its benefits and ways to achieve it. We'll then move on to strategies for ensuring workplace health; there are plenty of small actions that you can take when stuck behind that desk that will help your overall well-being.

Next we'll look at the concept of self-discipline, and consider methods to avoid loneliness and isolation, a big issue that affects many solo workers. We'll then discuss general health and wellness ideas and tips for freelancers, and discover ways in which you can improve your physical and emotional well-being.

Then we'll tackle the subject of community support—as a freelancer, you have an obligation not only to yourself and your clients, but to the wider community. We'll talk about ways to give back, which don't necessarily need to cost a lot to implement.

Speaking of community, every freelancer should also be looking at ways to help reduce his or her footprint on the planet, reducing our need for fossil fuels, and in turn reducing ways in which we damage the environment. We'll explore different methods of being green in your business and life.

Finally, we'll finish with an interview with a well-known speaker and expert on social media, knowledge management, web strategy, and information architecture, Stephen Collins; he'll discuss what actions he takes to look after himself and the world around him.

Looking After Yourself

In order that people may be happy in their work, these three things are needed: They must be fit for it. They must not do too much of it. And they must have a sense of success in it.
—John Ruskin, 1850

Much of the talk you'll hear with regard to work–life balance might give you the impression that all you need to do is ensure you don't work more than the daylight hours you're given—but this is rather simplistic. Ideally, you'll concentrate on various aspects of your life beyond your working hours, to achieve a good balance throughout your life.

This balance promotes some great benefits, including:

- a healthier and fitter you
- reduced stress levels
- increased sense of happiness and well-being
- social support
- balance of perspective
- further self-development
- greater emotional balance and improved self-esteem

You might start by planning activities outside of work hours, just like you do when scheduling your working week. An example is to set aside as little as half an hour of physical activity at the start of a working day; this can have a great effect on the rest of your day, making you feel more motivated and relaxed, and ready to deal with any hurdle you may face.

Allow for important "you time," too. This may seem like a luxury if you have a family or partner clamoring for your attention, but its importance to your health can't be overestimated—set aside regular time for yourself to savor and enjoy life, and don't cave in to feelings of guilt. Spend that couple of hours alone on activities you enjoy; mark the times out on your calendar and even set reminders, if this helps; it can be all too easy to put it off and think of your own needs as a low priority.

If you have few interests outside your area, consider broadening your horizons by taking up activities not related to your work—you might take an adult course in cooking, Spanish, or pottery, or seek out someone to play racquetball or chess with. Set aside part of your budget for these personal activities—this may seem hard at the start when you're potentially living from check to check, but what's the point of earning money if you don't spend a little on enhancing your life?

Many people also have religious or spiritual pursuits, such as taking time to go to church or temple, or even participating in volunteer services. You should avoid letting your work interfere with these times, as they are an important part of your sense of identity.

If you feel stressed, work on relaxation techniques such as meditation, yoga, or tai chi, or simply chill out with music or a good book—it's amazing what even a modest allowance of downtime can add to your productivity!

Caring for Yourself at Work

There are plenty of simple strategies to adopt during the workday to encourage a healthier you, and avoid that desk physique. An obvious one is to look at office ergonomics, which, as previously mentioned, goes far beyond the nicely shaped mouse. Look at your workspace layout. Does it invite a productive day, but allow plenty of opportunity for breaks? Do your monitors, chair, and desk suit your working habits? If not, make the changes—they're often a lot less expensive than you'd think.

Eating well is very important. Eat breakfast. Skipping the first meal of the day gives your metabolism nothing to start on, meaning that you'll feel lethargic and more likely to start eating sugar-laden snacks to get firing on all cylinders. If you can, prepare yourself a healthy fresh lunch each day and avoid falling into that easy junk food rut.

Fast food and most sodas on the market are loaded with sugar and high in calories, which means that the temporary sugar rush you'll feel from consuming them is followed by a very counter-productive sugar crash. Ensure your diet includes plenty of fresh fruit and vegetables, and replace high-sugar and high-fat snacks such as chocolate or chips with nuts and legumes— it makes great sense for both your longer-term health and your productivity.

Don't forget about that all-important water intake, either. Between 60 and 70% of your body is water, most of it contained in your blood, muscles, and organs; hence, you need constant replenishment. You should aim to drink a daily water quota based on your size: divide your body weight in pounds in half, and then drink that in ounces. For example, if you were 150 pounds (68kg), you should aim to drink 75 ounces of water (just over two liters) a day. Having a large bottle full of water on your desk encourages you to take a drink regularly—I often finish three large bottles in a day, without even realizing. This is a great way to avoid snacking as well!

Love your coffee? You're not alone—the whole web industry seems to be fueled by caffeine. There's no doubt that a strong coffee is a great pick-me-up; however, be conscious of your caffeine intake, and intersperse your espressos with healthier alternatives such as water or the occasional fruit juice. If you regularly drink more than four coffees or energy drinks in one day, I strongly recommend you cut down. Be aware that going cold turkey may lead to several days of headaches and other withdrawal symptoms.

If you smoke, seriously consider giving up. It may seem like a calmative, the better to counter the stresses of freelancing, but it isn't—and it *is* well and truly proven and documented that it's doing serious long-term damage to your body. Same with alcohol—social drinking might be relaxing and seem par for the course, but if you start noticing that you're drinking every day, it may be time to contain your consumption for the sake of both your body and your workload.

Maintaining Health and Wellness

In a world of fast-paced projects, looming deadlines, and late nights of working, it's far too easy to overlook spending time on your fitness and begin to lack awareness of your physical health.

You need to consciously work on avoiding that dreaded behind-a-desk physique. Start by ensuring that you take regular breaks, and try to integrate physical movement into them. Stand up from your chair every hour or so, and walk around your house or office. It's not a crime to stop for lunch and leave your desk. Go to your kitchen or another room, sit down and eat something healthy; consider a brisk five-minute walk at the start of your lunch break to get the blood flowing and the brain working at its best. This may seem like a waste of time when starting out, but you'll come back refreshed, awake, and likely more productive. It doesn't need to be half an hour or more—even five or ten minutes of brisk walking around the block or down your street will make you feel more alert and give you a small dose of fresh air and exercise. When taking phone calls, stand and stretch. This not only makes you sound more active to the other caller, but keeps you focused on the call, and not on your monitor.

When visiting a client's office for meetings, or going to a cafe to work, consider riding a bicycle or walking. If this isn't feasible, try driving or catching a bus, then stop a few blocks early and walk the rest of the way. When you reach your destination, look for opportunities to take the stairs and not the elevator. Consider buying or hiring a treadmill or exercise bike for the office or home. This way, you can burn calories while brainstorming, taking a mental break, or reading your mail.

Join a health club. There are gyms all over the globe, and there's likely to be one near you. Get into the routine of going there before starting your workday, or after work as a wind down. Even working out just twice a week for an hour or so makes a huge improvement to a desk-based worker. Furthermore, most people find that visiting a gym with a friend means you're more likely to keep the habit up. You could even make attendance competitive among local freelancers, just for some added incentive.

Try out yoga or meditation. These forms of exercise are very good for your mental health, which is an important part of a holistic approach to your overall well-being. This encourages you to be more focused and increases your mental energy levels. You might join think about joining a local sports team. Team sports are a great way to meet other people, and get fit while socializing. And there's always that networking opportunity—you may meet your next client there!

Take holidays! This is a hard task in the first year or two of starting out; however, you should plan to take the occasional vacation. It's great for you to switch off and tune out for a few days, and it's great for your partner or family to have you relaxed and spending time with them for a change. It needn't be long—perhaps start with long weekend getaways, and build upon these over time. And never feel guilty about these breaks, don't pine if you can't check your emails several times a day, and don't worry if your cell phone loses reception—you deserve the time out!

Having Self-discipline

Talent without discipline is like an octopus on roller skates. There's plenty of movement, but you never know if it's going to be forward, backwards, or sideways.
—H. Jackson Brown Jr.

In order to have all this time to spend on the golf course or at the shopping mall, you need to ensure that your work time is best utilized and deployed effectively. For the most part, attaining this productivity comes down to having a high level of self-discipline.

Those freelancers without self-discipline are the ones who can often be seen working weekends and way into every night. They're perpetually busy but seemingly unproductive—and they're the first to complain about their long hours.

We've covered many of these concepts earlier, but just to recap:

- Have regular working hours, and stick to them.

- Set time limits on household duties, so you don't end up spending a day on a procrastinative clean-up of the kitchen drawers rather doing than any billable work.

- Dress as though you're at an office—not necessarily in corporate gear, but comfortably and well. Dressing to impress, rather than in a style in which you wouldn't take out the trash, puts you in the right mind for work and encourages you to stay in work mode.

- Reduce distractions—don't answer your personal phone, avoid having friends over during work hours, and keep that TV and games console off. Remove computer games from your workhorse if you need to.

■ Keep up those after-hours social activities—if you find yourself canceling that yoga class or book group regularly, perhaps your scheduling needs an overhaul, or you need to turn down some work!

By maximizing productivity during your work hours, you'll be more relaxed in the knowledge that you've met all your deadlines when it's time to wind down. That, plus having more time to relax instead of working all-nighters to meet deadlines, will keep you in a better emotional and physical place.

Staying Connected

Life as a solo worker can be very rewarding, allowing you to work in an environment of your own creation, in the attire you feel most comfortable wearing. However, many people report that a big downside is the absence of regular contact with colleagues.

Isolation is a very real issue for freelancers, but there are a number of ways you can tackle this problem.

Consider sharing office space with other freelancers, or look for a coworking office nearby. Coworking is a fairly recent phenomenon, and it's really taking off. The idea is that small groups of people create a cooperative office. Although similar to a business incubator or serviced office, a coworking space normally encourages far more collaboration and skills crossover than would the usual serviced office. To find out more about coworking, take a look at the Coworking Community Blog[1] as well as the Coworking Wiki,[2] which features a massive list of coworking spaces already in existence around the world.

Another good remedy for feelings of isolation is to join groups of similar people, both online and offline. Industry associations and social networks can be a great escape mechanism, as well as a valuable means of exchanging valuable information and forming new friendships.

---

[1] http://blog.coworking.info/
[2] http://coworking.pbwiki.com/

Don't neglect those old workmates or other friends. Make a habit of seeing them regularly—having friends outside your work is a great way to take your mind off those work pressures.

Online, there are a number of forums and discussion lists that allow web professionals to communicate, no matter where they are located. Examples of these include:

SitePoint Forums (http://www.sitepoint.com/forums/)

> Frequented by an active community of web designers and developers, the Site-Point forums are very popular.

Web Developer Forums (http://www.webdeveloper.com/)

> Owned by internet.com, Web Developer Forums features forums on a wide range of topics related to web development.

Webmaster Forums (http://www.webmaster-talk.com/)

> With over 60,000 members, Webmaster Forums covers topics such as code, design, search engine optimization, and more.

As well as these online forums, and the many software and hardware user groups already established, there's a number of web industry groups that meet in the flesh on a regular basis. A short list of groups follows, but don't just take my word for it—ask other freelancers and search online for other groups near you.

BarCamp (http://www.barcamp.org/)

> The BarCamp movement is less an official organization than a collective of people across the globe who hold "un-conferences." Since the inception in August 2005, hundreds of BarCamps have been held in dozens of cities around the planet. Visit the web site for a current list of events.

Geek Dinners (http://geekdinner.co.uk/)

> Geek Dinners are London-based, semi-regular social evening events, organized by volunteers. Some previous dinners have seen some well-known industry figures present their wisdom over a meal or casual drink, so if you're in the area, do check them out.

Port80 (http://www.port80.asn.au/)

Port80 is an Australian web industry group that meets monthly in various cities, as well as presenting an active online forum. Run by volunteers, the meetings are free to attend, and have been operating since 2002.

Refresh (http://www.refreshingcities.org/)

Refresh is an informal web industry network that holds events throughout the US, as well as in Canada, Mexico, and the UK.

Web Design Meetup (http://webdesign.meetup.com/)

Web Design Meetup started and is hosted through the Meetup.com site, and is a loose group of events, often found at coffee shops or licensed venues in a number of countries around the world.

Web Standards Group (http://webstandardsgroup.org/)

Web Standards Group is a collective of web designers and developers who have a particular interest in web standards. They hold regular events in a few countries, as well as hosting a very active email mailing list.

Work@Jelly (http://www.workatjelly.com/)

Work@Jelly is a casual coworking get-together, now up and running in over 20 cities around the globe.

Sign up to your local group from the above list, and go along to an event—not only is it refreshing to be surrounded by people in a similar situation to yourself, but you may even find work and collaboration partners as well! At the very least, try to grab a coffee with fellow industry people once in a while—this gives you the ability to talk shop with those who know what XHTML or a PNG is, and can be great as a motivation boost.

 Throw Your Own Party

If there are no regular meet-ups within your area, consider organizing one. Many of the above networks encourage chapter creation, or you can go it alone and build your own monthly or quarterly industry event. It's even easier if you know a few other freelancers in your field who might be keen to help organize them.

Another method to help avoid loneliness is to work from a cafe or library, if possible. Assuming it has wireless Internet, and you have a laptop, you can easily spend a few hours over a couple of coffees at a table and at least get a change in surroundings once in a while. It may not prove to be a huge surge in social contact (and, let's face it, you *are* meant to be working), but it will help you to go beyond your own four walls and remember that other humans exist!

Thinking Beyond the Office

Looking after yourself extends to your involvement with others, as we've seen, and that doesn't stop with the loved ones who live in your house, or the few friends with whom you make a concerted effort to remain connected outside of work hours. There's a whole world out there beyond those four walls, and it's vital you remain engaged with it. You *can* use your services for good as well as profit; your ability to help others, and make a difference in the community, is a well-known ingredient of personal fulfilment and balance, which will boost your self-esteem and sense of happiness.

Then there's the increasingly question of the environment, and your place within it. Every day, we hear more and more worrying reports of what humankind is doing to the earth we share, and its increasingly unpredictable responses—while you're looking two weeks into the future toward looming deadlines, you need to remember that there's an even longer and infinitely larger view that too many people ignore as being beyond their control. It might seem daunting and difficult to even attempt making a difference, but there's really no excuse for anything other than environmentally friendly practices any more—and you may find that your business's environmental concern and sustainability becomes an increasing decision factor of clients choosing to work with you in the years to come.

Supporting the Community

I strongly believe every enterprise, no matter how large or small, has an obligation to do what it can for the wider community. One method that I've always supported is doing pro-bono work for charities and worthwhile causes.

Donating some of your time and expertise to a charity costs you very little, yet can make a massive difference to the recipient. It doesn't need to cost you much more than a few hours a month, and you'll feel great spending time on a worthwhile cause.

Remember that in addition to the payoff in warm fuzzy good-karma feelings, you're also opening yourself to new networking opportunities, which can certainly pay dividends. Think of the people who sit on the boards of most charitable organizations—they're typically business owners, entrepreneurs, and industry leaders as well, and it doesn't hurt to get your work in front of them.

Can't spare the time or want to help further? Consider making financial donations. Look for charities in your area that you believe need the funds, or get involved in programs such as One Percent for the Planet.[3] Alternatively, you can help spread prosperity to other communities by investing small amounts in businesses through micro-financing models, such as Kiva[4] or MicroPlace.[5] Look at any taxation benefits—speak to your accountant or taxation advisor, as financial contributions to charities can often reduce your taxable income or provide other financial benefits.

Then there's always equipment donations—many cities around the world have organizations that will collect old computer hardware, and then redistribute these to the needy—as web people, we often buy the latest gadgets and throw away equipment that we believe is defunct or obsolete for our purposes, but in actual terms still has plenty of life in it for other users. That said, if you're donating hard drives or computers, ensure you wipe off any data that may remain on them before handing them over. A privacy breach could wind up being very embarrassing and possibly damaging to your business or clients. Don't simply drop files into Trash—the disk should be over-written and then formatted, or to be especially sure, you could take the hard drive out and destroy it.

Being Green

Beyond the wider community beyond our office walls, there's the even larger planet we all inhabit. In recent years, more and more businesses are taking their obligations towards climate change, recycling, and environmental awareness far more seriously. We can all do our part to save the planet ourselves, and you'll find

---

[3] http://www.onepercentfortheplanet.org/
[4] http://www.kiva.org/
[5] https://www.microplace.com/

many of the following ideas are not only cheap or free to implement, they can also save you some significant money in the longer term.

Change your incandescent light bulbs to energy-efficient ones. These typically last much longer than traditional globes, and will save up to 80% on your electricity costs. Use LCD monitors instead of the old CRTs. Not only do they tend to be better, they also use a lot less power.

Turn off equipment when not using it. Powering down your computers and switching monitors off can make a big dent in your power bills, and are another small help towards reducing our fossil fuel usage. If you use a laptop, run it on battery for an hour or so each day. This is good for cycling the battery and reduces your mains power usage. This also goes for any air-conditioning or heating—turning the thermostat up or down just one degree can have a significant impact.

Purchase recycled paper for your office printer; even better, have any stationery, such as business cards, printed on 100% recycled stock—ask your printer about the options. Wherever possible, recycle your paper; print on both sides, or cut up previously printed paper and staple it together to use as handy notepads.

Figure 7.1. Look for the recycled symbol on your paper and plastic products

In turn, look for the recycled symbol on your paper and plastic products, which should look something like Figure 7.1, to see if and how they should be recycled. The more you can recycle, the less strain on the environment. This works the other way too—second-hand furniture is not only cheap, it is also great for the environment—look in local thrift stores for your next desk or chair.

Embrace the paperless office philosophy, and avoid printing out documents or emails where possible. Ask all of your suppliers to invoice you electronically. This saves postage and paper—and provides you with a handy archiving system. In turn, send electronic invoices, and reduce paper consumption and use of postal resources. Most clients are starting to prefer this tactic anyway, and emailing an invoice means the client has it a day or more before a postal invoice would arrive. (Make sure that these are all backed up for the appropriate archiving time, depending on your local taxation and business laws.)

Stick a No Junk Mail sign on your letterbox. The US uses at least 68 million trees each year to produce 17 billion catalogues and 65 billion pieces of direct mail, according to the American Forest and Paper Association. Read your news online, rather than from newspapers. Here's a shocking statistic to put this in perspective: the North Carolina Office of Waste Reduction and Recycling calculates that it takes 75,000 trees to print just one Sunday edition of the *New York Times*.

If you choose to send Christmas cards to clients, buy recycled paper ones from your favorite charity—you'll be making a statement to your recipients, as well as supporting the work of local organizations. Instead of sending paper Christmas cards, send electronic ones. You can brand them and make them fun, and they also show the kind of work you can do!

Buy rechargeable batteries for any battery-powered devices. This can save you lots of money over a long time, and saves you throwing dead batteries in the bin. Look for a cell phone recycling program, when upgrading your phone—it can be put to far better use than sitting in your drawer collecting dust.

When going to meetings, try to catch public transport. This is not only smarter for greenhouse gases, but keeps you fit at the same time. Make sure you give yourself ample time to get there and back, so you don't run late! Avoid old-school postal services and couriers, which use lots of fuel, and encourage clients to use email or FTP to share files. There are some substantial cost savings in this practice, as well. Reduce the number of airline flights you take, or at least choose an airline that has a carbon offset program—this adds a few dollars to your ticket, and helps "pay" for the emissions you use.

Consider the energy ratings or energy stars of appliances when making that next equipment purchase. Buy green power for your home or office from your electricity provider. See the Energy Efficiency and Renewable Energy[6] web site for details and a handy map, if you're in the US.

Use suppliers that are environment-aware. Many companies are now promoting their environmental programs on their web sites and in marketing material. For example, there are many green-power hosting facilities appearing around the globe. Keep a lookout for fair trade alternatives for your purchases. Coffee and tea from Fair Trade suppliers are a great example of this.

Read the great eco-blog, Tree Hugger.[7] The site is jam-packed with great ideas and discussion. Encourage clients and suppliers to embrace these tips, by including the occasional environmental tip in your electronic newsletter or blog. Organize to offset your carbon emissions by planting trees. This not only helps save the world, it's also a great marketing opportunity for you to promote to your clients.

Interview with Stephen Collins

Stephen Collins is the Founder and Chief Troublemaker at acidlabs.[8] Recognized as one of Australia's leading proponents of participatory culture, Web 2.0, Enterprise 2.0, and social networking, he is driven by a need to help people and organizations effect change in their capacity to retain, distribute, and share knowledge.

He has extensive consulting experience for a diverse client base across government and private enterprise, and has expertise in social media and networking, knowledge management, web strategy, information architecture, and user experience. He is a sought-after speaker and expert for media, conferences, and seminars in Australia and internationally, including Office 2.0[9] in San Francisco and Interesting South[10] in Sydney.

---

[6] http://www.eere.energy.gov/greenpower/

[7] http://www.treehugger.com/

[8] http://www.acidlabs.org/

[9] http://www.o2con.com/

[10] http://www.interestingsouth.com/

Figure 7.2. The acidlabs web site

I caught up with Stephen, and asked him a few questions about what he does to look after himself.

What is your experience of keeping a work–life balance, and what has worked best for you?

Work–life balance is a major issue, and I have a number of practices that have put structure into the things I do that help. Of course, there are times when I don't achieve balance at all, and spend too much time working. But overall, these things help.

First, I have a defined work start time. If I'm working from home, which is about 70% of the time, I don't start working until my wife, Alli, has left for work and my daughter, Hannah, is at school. Sometimes I get Hannah to school—and walk the dog at the same time—other times, Alli takes her. It kind of depends on how organized we are.

Second, my day ends very specifically. When I collect Hannah from after school care (if it's my turn) and Alli is home, it's tools down.

Once we're all home we have a very explicit focus on family time—cooking dinner, discussing our day, watching some news, reading together, getting homework done. Once Hannah's in bed, I can go back to work if I need to. Other times I'll spend some time relaxing. I take my cue from Alli; if she's studying or working, I often will as well.

Working for yourself can often be isolating—how do you combat this?

It *can* be very isolating! My clients are largely not in Canberra, where I live, so travelling to work with them is fairly frequent. That gets me out and about.

When I'm at home in Canberra, I make a point of trying to get to things—WSG, IA Cocktail Hour, and the like—as well as more ad hoc stuff like coffee with colleagues and industry friends or an impromptu Twitter meet-up.

If I didn't do these things, I'd certainly go stir crazy. Weeks where I'm particularly busy can be a real challenge. I tend to get grumpy and isolated and need to be kicked (metaphorically) in order to come back to reality.

What do you believe are some worthwhile goals, when we talk about growing an ethical business?

I think our businesses need strong ethics. I've seen too many freelancers take on work or claim to be able to do work that they're not qualified for.

I made a point in January this year of publishing a manifesto about the way I work. It's attracted a little attention and it's something I'm proud of. In it, I address issues such as my expectations of myself and my clients. In particular, things like working on projects I believe in, not taking on work I can't for reason of skills or availability, realism, and not over-promising.

I think these are really important issues, and I hope it differentiates me from some of the other players out there. In particular, I'd like to be taking little percentages out of some of the really big consulting companies. Having worked for a fairly large consulting firm in the past, the account execs in them have a tendency to promise the world without thinking about what's achievable or even what the consultant they're sending is capable of. That sort of stuff really annoys me.

If you could give only one tip for someone starting freelancing, what would you suggest?

Do it. Find someone who's prepared to pay you enough money on a contract, doing what you want to do, to cover your bills for at least six months and jump. You won't regret it. Six months at a time was my promise to Alli when I started. If I couldn't get work every six months; I'd go back to looking for work as someone's employee. Eighteen months in, and it doesn't look like slowing.

There are lots of other things I could suggest—a *really* good accountant and business advisor that has lots of small business clients is probably the next most important!

Case Study

Emily

Emily has come a long way since she threw in that job in media and went out on her own. Her confidence has risen, her contacts have increased, and life is good to her, even if the earnings work out to be about the same, or even slightly less, once her taxes and accounts have been sorted for the first year. One issue that Emily never anticipated is the amount of stress she'd feel, waiting for those checks to clear, clients to approve work, and never quite knowing where she'll get her work the next month.

The benefits of Emily's new lifestyle outweigh this, though, with her running around the park most mornings instead of rushing to the office with a coffee in her hand. Emily feels fitter and happier than she has in years, and is positive that with a concentrated effort on keeping a good balance, this pattern will continue. Friends and family often ask her why she works late some evenings, but Emily is happy to do so, knowing she trades off the occasional afternoon to go to cafes with friends or spend the day with family—this also helps to prevent feelings of isolation.

Although she feels successful, Emily doesn't have much money left over after all the bills, and setting aside a little extra in profit. Rather than donating money to charities, Emily has offered her services to a local children's health association, and is working with another freelancer to build a new web site. The teamwork has proven to be good, they complement each other's skill sets well, and they've already pitched on a few small projects as a team.

Emily still spends a large portion of her time working out of her clients' offices—so her home office, although probably not as environmentally friendly as it could be, isn't actually used more than half the week.

Jacob

The last few months have been huge for Jacob. He's gone from being a freelancer to being an employer of sorts, taking on a few contractors part-time and per project to help him cope with the work. He has paid back his parents' initial loan, and feels confident that he will stay cash flow positive.

Jacob is still in charge of all the design work, but he has accepted that his strengths are in client contact and design direction, so is happy to give the other work, such as design cutouts and heavier developer work, to freelance colleagues. He is considering moving into a small office to allow him to have staff work in with him, without feeling like they're invading his home. As such, he has already started looking for second-hand desks, and is keeping an eye out for a reasonably priced office to work from within easy reach of home.

Although Jacob is bringing in the money and feeling that he has made a great decision, he certainly isn't taking care of himself. Every week, he works at least three evenings into the night, and has takeaway meals for most dinners. He has let his gym membership lapse, because he feels he's too busy to go. Jacob is starting to realize the cost of this lifestyle, though—he's missed deadlines, slept in, and feels more stressed than ever.

One of his first ten clients was a charity, and although Jacob gave them a break on the price, he didn't offer to do the work for free. Now that he is bringing in more income, he feels that it is time for him to do his bit for them, and has donated 5% of last month's earnings, which he hopes to continue to do with other charities in the future.

Summary

I hope by now it's obvious that there's more to freelance life than working twenty-hour days and drinking copious amounts of coffee. A great work–life balance is the key to a happier lifestyle, which results in better productivity and general well-being.

It's important to not just look after your physical health, but also look at your mental health—stay happy by avoiding isolation, maintaining extracurricular hobbies, and keeping a lid on stress. Self-discipline is a big part of the equation. You need to be able to focus exclusively on work during your business day and work on relaxing outside of this time. Letting work and life times blur ends up a disaster, with you never switching off from work and not being as productive as you could be.

Success isn't just about financial rewards, either—we also looked at ways in which we can share our success with the community around us, through donations, volunteering, and being aware of the impact we have on the world. That led us into a discussion about the environment. The world needs more of its inhabitants to care about the environment, if we want to see our descendants enjoy it like we can. We looked at strategies, both large and small, which we can adopt to help this planet of ours and the people who live on it.

So where from here? What does the future hold for you, now that you are established as a freelancer?

Where to from Here?

Congratulations! You've built a successful freelancing business. Naturally, you'll now start to ask yourself where to go from here. You've reached decision time. What's the next step, the further challenge?

The first part of forward progress is often the hardest—you need to make some big decisions around longer-term plans. Are you looking to build a company with staff and, with any luck, a larger turnover? Or do you wish to stay solo and increase profits by being choosier about the projects you accept?

Perhaps you've even decided that although freelancing was great for the last few months or years, it's time for you to get out. This decision isn't something to fear or be ashamed of; it isn't failure, it's a change in lifestyle. Be honest with yourself about your gut feeling—freelancing may not have given you the career you were hoping for, or it may not have provided the lifestyle you expected at the outset. Perhaps you miss the stability that a salaried job for an employer allows. Or perhaps you've been so successful that you're feeling overworked, but now have the resources to allow you to look for an escape plan—you might consider downsizing to a career path with less responsibility and stress.

The first option we examine is to remain as a solo freelancer, as you've been doing up to this point. Perhaps everything's ticking along nicely; there's no reason for you to change, and no need for any hard-and-fast decisions right now, either.

The second alternative is to get out of freelancing. Maybe the life just wasn't for you—and don't panic, there's always a way to return to employment elsewhere. However, what to do with those clients? We look at taking your clients with you, selling your clients to a third party, or referring your clients to use another freelancer or service provider.

The third option here is obvious: to build your business from being just a team of one by enlisting other people and expanding your business. We'll discuss the outsourcing model, and chat about its advantages and disadvantages. We'll then take a look at virtual or coworking teams, and discuss what these entail. We will also discuss taking on part-time, casual, or full-time employees, and what you need to consider before taking the plunge. It's a big step, so you need to have all the facts.

We'll also discuss how you can avoid skill rot; this can be a very real problem, especially for freelancers. Then, we look in for the final time on our case study pair, Jacob and Emily, and bid them farewell.

Staying Solo

Making the conscious decision to stay solo and concentrate on staying a freelancer is well worth considering. Many people don't relish the idea of the pressure or responsibility of having employees, and dread returning to working for someone else. It may sound like that old "the grass is always greener" adage, but many people who are now employers often dream of being freelancers again!

There's no reason, if you're already doing well, to have to take on employees or contractors to increase your profits and earn more. In many instances, it is simply a process and habit of becoming more selective with the projects you take on, and having a good stable of other freelancers to whom you can refer your overflow work.

You can gain a better understanding of where you make your money by looking at recent projects, and scrutinizing the hours you spend versus the income you make. If you do this for a good chunk of your time, say the previous six months, you'll be confident enough to identify where the profit comes from, and where the hassles or even the losses crop up.

Go back to that business plan we used at the very start, and update what constitutes your ideal client and ideal projects. You'll often be surprised to find what you thought was profitable and what actually *is* profitable are two very different things.

All this talk of money, however, is trivial if your lifestyle is suffering. Your well-being cannot be underestimated, and it's no good concentrating only on the financially profitable activities if they're the ones that you experience as a depressing burden.

Once you've worked out an analysis of your recent history, as well as your own feelings about the sorts of projects you enjoy, what you should be concentrating on will become clear. Now it is time to find those around you who can do the rest. You've probably already built some partnerships and links with other freelancers—it's time to really use these relationships by referring all projects which don't fit your ideal project profile to them.

It's always scary and a little sad to turn away work, but if you've done your analysis properly, you should feel confident that your time is better spent on high-earning or high-satisfaction activities, instead of those projects that are a pain to deal with, or even loss-making.

The art of leadership is saying no, not yes. It is very easy to say yes.
—Tony Blair, UK Prime Minister, 1997–2007

Be careful though—you don't want to turn away the majority of your current influx of work to chase an elusive "perfect world" project. It's best to think of it as a transition of your workload over a realistic time frame, unless you've got a queue of willing perfect clients with exciting projects outside your door!

Retiring from Freelancing

Perhaps you dream of a more stable employment situation, and you've been considering throwing in the freelance towel and going back to full-time employment. It seems that mcst freelancers do feel this way at one time or another, and they either shake it off as just a transitory mood or feel reluctant to leave freelancing because they believe that to be an admission of failure.

Let's straighten out one misconception. Leaving freelance life to return to employment is *not* a sign of personal failure. Freelance life is hard. It can be very hard. Juggling projects with the rest of your life, as well as keeping the finances flowing so you can support yourself and any dependants, is a tricky skill to perfect, and not something everyone can handle. The lifestyle can be tough, too; late nights, early starts, and the self-discipline of switching on and off can be very stressful.

If you've tried freelancing, you've learned plenty, and you managed to stay above water for this long, be proud of your achievements!

In fact, I had two attempts at freelancing before going back a third time and making a real go of it. Looking back, I have no regrets returning to a job; the lessons I learned in both freelancing and working as an employee during those periods helped me immensely the third and final time I took up freelancing.

Looking After Your Clients

As part of the migration to full-time employment, you may have clients or projects that require a new home. It's important you take the ethical route here, and support the transition to another freelancer or company. You can take your clients to your new employer, you could sell the client base as an ongoing concern, or, if neither of these options is available to you, you could refer them to other freelancers or small businesses for a fee.

Let's look at these choices in a little more detail.

Bringing Your Clients with You

If you're shopping around for a position in the same field as your freelance work, or have already landed a job, you may be in a position to offer your employer a new client base—and your clients a new home—as long as you learn the ground rules.

It's important to consider if the new company you're working for will suit your current client base. Perhaps the charges are far higher than your clients were used to with you, or the service offerings are considerably different to what you provided on your own. If there's any doubt, it's normally better for both parties to avoid bringing them together.

However, if the prospects are all positive, you'll need to be very honest and up-front with both your new employer and your clients. You need to ensure that your new employer understands that some of these clients may go elsewhere, and that some of these clients may turn out to be difficult or unprofitable within this new environment. Make sure to stress that you are simply introducing them, and not vouching for their longer-term profitability. You don't want one of your clients to become a nightmare for your new boss, and for you to be judged unfairly as a consequence.

The same goes for your clients. There's a strong likelihood that you'll be obliged to relinquish control over how the relationships with your clients are managed to someone else in the organization. This is as it should be, but you need to make sure your clients understand that they are your new employer's clients, and no longer yours. The last thing you want is to find yourself working nights and weekends to appease clients whom you thought you were handing over. There's still the risk is that a client will be dissatisfied by something or someone at the new organization, and hold you responsible. I'd suggest being very straight with them from the very start, and stating that you're only offering them an introduction to the new employer as a favor for both sides.

Selling Your Clients

Depending on how many clients you have, and what sort of income they bring in, your client list may be an asset worth selling. It's fairly common for larger businesses to sell client lists if they shut down an area of their business, or even sell their entire client base if they're winding up. As a freelancer, you've possibly built a reasonable list of clients that may be attractive to other freelancers, or more likely, larger businesses in the same industry.

The main issue for a freelancer selling a client list lies in the value of the ongoing business. As a freelancer, most of your clients are with you not only for your talent and skills, but also because they've developed a personal connection with you. As such, prospective purchasers may place a value on your client list that's far less than your own.

We've discussed recurring income, which is what a buyer would be most interested in. Any ongoing profitable contract arrangements, hosting plans, or domain name registrations will have the most worth in the eyes of the buyer, while ad-hoc service work will be worth the least. This is especially the case if the client has had no recent interaction with you.

You'll also improve your chances of a sale, and possibly improve the selling price, if you offer your willingness to participate in a transition process, to help with introductions and a smooth handover. Given the risk that your clients may jump ship and go elsewhere as a result of the changes, it's important that you do what you can to ensure stability, and a smooth process, for both the buyer as well as your clients. This introduction may be a well-written letter to all of your clients, or a telephone call, or coordination of a physical meeting. This will depend on how many clients you have, and what they are worth to the prospective buyer.

 Be Careful Where You Advertise

Be very careful not to advertise this sale somewhere where clients will read it. They may start to feel like cattle being sold from a farm.

You should also discuss this with your accountant, who may suggest contacting a business broker as well. You'll likely need to show some financial records to prove that these clients have brought in the income, so you'll need to work closely with your accountant to present the right figures.

A professional business broker, who specializes in freelancers or the creative industries, can be very helpful to you. They'll have a far better comprehension of how to value your client base, maximizing the resulting sale price. Brokers may also have a plan for marketing your client list, and even know people within their networks who may be interested. They also do much of the legwork, such as meeting prospective buyers and collating the right information from both yourself and your accountant.

Most business brokers tend to work for a percentage of the final sales price—remember that this is usually negotiable, so don't be reluctant to discuss a price.

Referring Your Clients

If none of the above options suits you, consider referring your clients to other freelancers or businesses that you know and trust—as a last resort. Irrespective of whether you believe you'll never go back to freelancing, or ever see these clients again, it's still important that you consider your reputation. Simply closing the doors and walking away is only an option if you've got zero projects on and no clients who rely on you for maintenance. This is a rare situation, so do the right thing and find a good alternative for your clients.

If you can, compile a list of freelancers who would be the best fit for your client base. You probably already have other freelancers you know through networking, or with whom you've partnered on previous projects. These are the ideal candidates, if you have a fair idea of their skill sets and abilities. Then, approach them and organize a face-to-face meeting over a coffee or lunch to discuss in more detail. Your first objective here should be to find a freelancer or group who can service your clients to the same standards than yourself, and have similar skills to offer them.

You may also like to consider the opportunity to make a passive income by suggesting an agreement where you get a modest percentage of the business these clients bring in for the first 12 months. If you do reach an agreement, make sure you get it in writing. This should detail percentages, restrictions on trade—whether payments are only for new work, recurring work, and so on—and payment terms, such as every month, quarter, or once the project is complete.

Much of this agreement will need to be based on honesty, however—you aren't in a position to have a really clear understanding of what work you've given someone else, especially once clients start dealing directly with them.

Building That Business!

You've made a success of this freelance life so far, you've looked at the various options, and now you're looking to expand. Congratulations! You've done well to come so far—but now there are more decisions to make. There are many options for expanding the team beyond yourself.

We'll take a look at the choices ahead of you, along with a few notes on the hurdles and concerns some of these may bring. Irrespective of which path you take from here, you can pat yourself on the back for your achievements, secure in the knowledge that you're building your business and creating even further success!

Outsourcing

The term **outsourcing** often brings with it a sense of ethical dilemma: hiring people from third-world countries for a measly sum; running your remote teams like a sweat shop. In fact, it needn't be anything like this scenario. Outsourcing is essentially hiring someone from outside your business to do skilled work for you. You could outsource to a housemate, a freelancer you know from that local cafe, or someone on the other side of the planet.

There are a number of reasons you may prefer to outsource work rather than have a contractor who works from your office, or hire a casual, part-time, or full-time employee. Benefits of outsourcing over having in-house talent can include some of the following:

reduced costs
Instead of hiring a permanent employee, and have periods of unbillable activity, you can reduce these by hiring only when you need to. If you're comfortable dealing with contractors from afar, there are significant cost savings available by outsourcing to less wealthier countries, where expectations of hourly rates are considerably lower than you'll find locally.

wider range of skills available
Rather than hiring one or two employees or contractors, who have their own limited skill sets, you can pick from a broad pool of available contractors. We'll be discussing online services, which feature hundreds of thousands of individually skilled contractors across the globe.

easily increase or decrease work force
It's an inescapable fact: workload varies. One week you'll have nothing, and the next you'll be swimming in projects. Having a successful outsourcing system allows you to expand and shrink your contractor workforce as required.

increase your work capacity
It goes without saying that the more hours you can bill per week, the more your turnover will increase, and higher your profits rise. Outsourcing is another method of helping to build your nest egg faster!

The above advantages may be very appealing; however, there are also disadvantages to outsourcing your projects, especially to contractors in remote locations:

trust and privacy issues

Trust and privacy concerns ring especially true if the contractor with whom you're dealing is remotely based. All of the legal contracts and agreements in the world won't really help you with a dishonest contractor halfway around the world.

You may even be restricted from subcontracting any of the work out, if you're under a Non-Disclosure Agreement or similar legal contract.

quality control issues

There will always be the prospect of quality control issues with anybody you employ. Since contractors tend to spend only a short period of time working with you, they have less motivation to ensure their work is always the best it can be, especially if it's likely to be a one-off job.

You can also run into trouble with maintenance if you have one person code the system, and another perform maintenance and tweaks a year later. Reading other people's code, especially if it's poorly written, can end in confusion and major rewriting.

communication barriers

If your communication is restricted to telephone and email, you need to prepare yourself for some communication issues. This can be even more exasperating if your primary spoken languages are not the same, and small nuances between dialects are lost. With a lack of non-verbal communication cues, such as tone of voice, facial expressions, or body language, you could easily misinterpret each other. We've all had emails in the past that have been taken the wrong way, haven't we?

Depending on the difference in time zone for further isolated contractors, you may find that your night is their workday and vice versa. This can actually be a good thing at times, but in general I've experienced it as a barrier and not as a benefit.

Given that your client is likely not to know you've subcontracted the work out, you'll be expected to right any urgent issues quickly—which can be hard if the person who originally built them is asleep or unreachable.

 Check Local TIme

To see the current time of most major cities at a glance, just check out Time-andDate.com's World Clock.[1] This can circumvent those midnight telephone calls, or frustration when someone doesn't answer your instant messenger request.

legal issues

You need to consider legal issues, such as confidentiality and copyright. If the contractor is within your state, you have a good chance of resolving any disputes through the legal system. However, if the contractor is on the other side of the world, there's little chance that any legal jurisdiction will cover both parties.

Laws can differ dramatically from country to country and even state to state, so make sure you research and understand the differences. It's very difficult to claim copyright infringements or stop an unethical contractor from reusing their code or designs, and it's even harder to enforce any confidentiality if there's little or no threat of a lawsuit.

ethical issues

There are many sides to every story, and using remote contractors from countries that have cheaper employees is a sensitive ethical issue. On one side, some people say it at least offers people who are less fortunate the potential to earn an income, and on the other, it is argued to be exploitive and insensitive to local cultural or community requirements.

You should explore both sides of the debate; there are hundreds of blog posts and articles dedicated to this topic. Make your own decisions, and be prepared to stick by them.

---

[1] http://www.timeanddate.com/worldclock/

Start Small

If you do hire a contractor, start them off with a small project. This way, you can test their skills and ability to do the work, yet not risk a large project or client to this acid test.

So, you've weighed up the pros and cons of outsourcing, and believe you'll have a try at outsourcing some work. If you don't know of anybody suitable to do the work, you can use your networks, as we've discussed in previous chapters, or you could look online.

There are a number of online services available for posting advertisements and creating outsourcing relationships. The following are just a few of these:

Elance (http://www.elance.com/)
Elance is broader than the web industry, with projects for legal, finance, administration, writing, engineering, and more.

Get a Freelancer (http://www.getafreelancer.com/)
Get a Freelancer is geared towards the web industry, and general IT solutions.

oDesk (http://www.odesk.com/)
oDesk covers a broad range of industries and professions.

Scriptlance (http://www.scriptlance.com/)
Scriptlance is designed to help find web designers and developers.

99designs (http://99designs.com/)
99designs enables you to run contests where designers compete to create designs to meet your needs. It's a good way to make contact with designers and form outsourcing relationships.

 ## Do Your Research

Spend some time reading other job advertisements before placing your own. Determine, if possible, at the amount of responses each post has had, and attempt to determine what worked and didn't work about the advertisement, which will help you craft your own.

When you're ready to kick off a project with a remote contractor, ensure you offer documentation that's as detailed as possible. Cover every potential issue imaginable, so there's less chance of wrong assumptions or miscommunications later. If something isn't explicitly addressed or written out in detail, it's all too likely to be missed.

Be frank and up-front about your expectations with privacy and deliverables, and when you hope to see the final product. Feel free to include a legal agreement for both parties to sign, concerned with keeping the work confidential, and insisting they don't approach your client directly.

When you believe you've found the right contractor, ask for examples of their previous work, as well as contact details so you can make reference checks. Test their communication skills, especially if they're working remotely and you expect to rely on telephone and email as your primary communication tools. The biggest failure of many people undertaking outsourcing is that they fail to make reference checks, do not check their candidates' skills, and simply take their word for everything.

Joining a Virtual Team

You've possibly had a small taste already of what a coworking or **virtual team** can offer. A person with complementary skills to yours may have ask you to be involved in a project. A virtual team, as its name suggests, is a group of people who interact mostly via electronic means (be it email, phone, instant messenger, Skype, and the like) and probably only ever meet face to face occasionally, if at all.

These teams often come together from geographically diverse locations and time zones to produce collaborative work, be it single projects or a more formal and longer-lasting agency-type arrangements. Sometimes, however, they may even be working out of the same offices, such as the coworking situations covered in previous chapters.

There are some great benefits for participants in virtual teams:

- There are no travel costs, as participants usually work from home.
- The working model is mostly independent of time zones.
- Multiple skills are available, without all the overheads of hiring permanent employees.
- Team members can be recruited from anywhere, not just locally.

Shared sales resources mean that you can share opportunities amongst the team.

There are equally some downsides to virtual teams:

- The lack of face-to-face communication often cause communication issues.
- Team members lack the monitoring they would have in an office.
- It doesn't suit individuals who lack self-discipline.
- New technologies, such as video conferencing equipment, may be required.

The easiest way to launch a virtual team is to use your existing contacts to find the right people. You should be striving for a situation where you're all bringing work to the team, and sharing opportunities among yourselves. For example, you may be a developer who's part of a team that includes a designer and a project manager with whom you can share your projects. They're there when you need design or project management resources, and in turn, the designer and project manager bring their projects to you in a reciprocal arrangement.

 Get Connected

Use instant messenger or a service like IRC (Internet Relay Chat) or CampFire[2] to have private round-table real-time discussions once a week, depending on time zones and workload.

This doesn't always work, so you need to be prepared for these arrangements to suddenly change. Virtual teamwork is like any good relationship, and you need to base it on great communication and trust. Be up-front with what you hope to achieve from the team, and don't be shy about letting other team members know when they have negatively (or, importantly, positively!) impacted you in some way.

If you do have a fairly established team, and you're all local, consider pitching in and setting up an office between you. If everyone is equally responsible for the rent and office, this situation can work out really well. Be aware, however, that shared offices can be noisy.

There's no reason to limit yourself to just one developer and one designer, either. There will be projects that require more than one pair of development hands, and

[2] http://www.getcampfire.com/

other times where two designers can be of great benefit. If you can, always have more than one person with the same skills.

Considering Staff

It's great that you've reached the point of even considering staff! This indicates that you've grown to a size where you can choose to either stay overworked and do it all yourself, or take on other people to help with the workload. This is an exciting situation to be in. Before making the leap to hiring full-time employees, though, you'll need to make many decisions and consider many options before you go and place that advertisement.

Having a permanent employee costs more than their basic salary. There are insurances, such as worker compensation, as well as superannuation, payroll taxes, and other sickness and annual leave benefits. Then there's the equipment, such as computer hardware and software, desk, chair, and telephone handset. You'll likely also need to to provide workplace amenities you mightn't have had when it was just you working from home. Add your time in training and managing them, and the pressure of having to keep another person fully occupied. The money spent on an employee works out to be anywhere from one-and-a-half times to twice as much as their gross salary, especially if they're your first.

What you really need to consider most is the ability to get the employee fully utilized and paying for themself as quickly as possible (we'll work on them actually earning money for you after that). If you believe you really only need someone one or two days per week, why take the risk of hiring a full-time employee, hoping you can find them enough work to cover those other three days? See if you can find someone who can start part-time or casual, and then increase their hours as the workload grows, if they're keen.

You should consider the other options first. There's the virtual team and outsourcing models we've just spoken about, and then there's the contractor, part-time, or casual employment arrangements. Consider hiring contractors on a per-project basis. This reduces your exposure to cost blowouts (especially if they agree to a set timeline and hours), and minimizes your administration overhead, if you have one large project to put them on.

Be careful to not promise anything you're unable to guarantee, though. It's fine to say you hope to make them full-time in the future, but you'll raise their hopes if you say they'll be full-time within ten weeks or some other fixed time period, and they make their own plans based on this promise. If this doesn't happen, you'll have a disgruntled employee on your hands, which can make life difficult.

Hiring Staff

If you do decide to hire staff, irrespective of whether it's a full-time, part-time, or casual basis, you need to clearly define the role for both your sake and theirs. This makes it easier for you to write an advertisement, as well as rate applicants against defined criteria, and allows candidates the opportunity to understand exactly who you're looking for.

You should provide as much detail as possible about the skills and knowledge required for the position, as well as the expected duties. Don't be afraid to include beneficial personality traits as well as desired previous experience or education minimums, if required. Be careful to not expect the world, though; you may need to trim back some of the requirements for the position when you advertise it, if you attract no interest.

Include a Trial Period

Ensure that you can legally include a trial or probation period in the employment contract. This can save you a huge headache if the person turns out to be no good, and you need to terminate their employment quickly.

During the interview, if they are indeed to be your first employee, you'll likely be selling yourself to them as much as the other way around. You need to make sure that the candidate feels that they can trust you, and have a belief in what you're embarking on.

An interview is not just about you talking. Take the time to actively listen and ask probing questions to gain a sense of their personality and work attitude. Make sure you also ask questions about how they would deal with specific work situations, and ask them to self-evaluate their own specific skills, when it comes to software or particular skills that you require.

Observe body language and non-verbal communication, as well as their appearance and communication skills. Make sure to take detailed notes as well, either during the interview or immediately afterwards. If you're interviewing a number of people over a few days, you'll find that your memories start to blur, and your recollections a week later when the time comes to decide won't be as sharp and reliable.

Managing Staff

So, you've found that right person with the skills and talent you need—congratulations! The management of other people is a skill and craft that is indeed a subject worthy of a book all on its own. You take on responsibilities not only in being the big boss, but also in the way you end up wearing the title of coach, mentor, leader, counselor, and chief motivator. It can be daunting to be responsible for the careers and livelihoods of others; yet at the same time many people find managing other people rewarding and interesting.

You'll find that you need to pick up skills along the way, and that you'll spend the rest of your life refining your management techniques. The thousands of how-to-manage-people books and web sites are testament to the constant demand and yearning for better management techniques and tips. You'll quickly find that you must juggle the needs of the business with the needs of the individual and the team. You'll also have to pick up skills for managing conflict and interpersonal issues, and the legal requirements around having employees; taxes, benefits, superannuation, insurance—the list goes on.

A very beneficial skill to possess is to be able to determine what motivates your team, and how you can keep them interested and suitably motivated. This is far from being about salary; in fact, many employee surveys find that financial remuneration is not the main decision-maker for an employee considering a job change.

Methods for attraction and motivation of your staff can include:

- challenging, exciting work
- job security
- respect and recognition
- opportunity for advancement
- fun, interesting workplace
- flexible work times

Then there are the softer benefits, such as regular social events, good coffee and tea facilities, comfortable chairs to relax in at lunchtime, and so on. Creating an environment that has a careful balance between productive and casual is essential, and equally as important as ensuring that you treat people with respect and reward them with competitive salary conditions and other benefits.

Use the position description used for advertising the position as a method for conducting regular performance reviews. You need to ensure that you regularly take the time to communicate with the employee about where they excel, and where their development areas lie. Don't forget to praise their efforts, and ensure that you're clear with your expectations. Much angst is caused by not being absolutely clear when defining your expectations of the processes and output.

 Be Sincere

Be sincere with praise. It's utterly pointless to put a reminder in your diary to say "Thanks, Mary!" every Tuesday at lunchtime. This will come across sounding false, and is almost as unproductive as not praising the person at all.

Be aware of all the legislation and taxation laws in your area, when it comes to being an employer. You need to make sure, at a bare minimum, that you meet all legislated requirements, for the peace of mind of both you and your staff.

As for terminating a staff member's employment, make sure that you've given them ample time and opportunity to rectify any behavior or development areas, and seek legal advice prior to the sacking; many legal issues arise as a result of a wrongful termination, so it's better to be safe than sorry.

If you do need to let someone go, or have someone resign, remember not to make it personal. It's hard not to, when you are such a small business, but there are a multitude of reasons somebody may leave your employ, and most of them have nothing to do with anything you've done.

Avoiding Skill Rot

Skill rot is a very real problem for everyone in the web industry, and particularly for freelancers. You experience skill rot when your skill levels remain the same, while the expected skill levels required from a person in your position keeps increasing, leaving you behind.

This is an industry where there's always a hundred new things to learn. You need to keep improving your skills, keep up-to-date with technology, learn new development techniques, and be across the whole tide of new methods of building the Web. Having said that, you also need to choose your skills path wisely. In early days of freelancing, I spent way too much time learning skills that I rarely needed or could easily outsource, instead of spending that precious time selling my services or completing projects.

It has to be said that standing still in this industry is akin to retiring. So what can we do to make sure we stay on top of the necessary skills we need, in order to be effective in what we do and successful at freelancing?

First, determine what skills are you hoping to keep up-to-date. These may be project management, design, development, front end code, server administration; whatever they are, list them in order of your priorities.

Now, go out and find blogs and other online resources that cover these areas. Ideally, seek out ones that are concerned with remaining at the forefront of that particular area of expertise; this way, you can keep an eye out for new programming languages and frameworks or techniques that pop up. Make sure you subscribe to their RSS feeds, and make it a habit to either skim the headlines each day, or put aside an hour or two every week to research and browse what's out there on the Web.

Once you've found a skills area that you'd like to examine more closely, look for online tutorials, books, or articles on the subject. You may even find online courses on the subject, and if you're lucky, offline courses near you as well. If you have a suitable project coming up, try to use that new technique in your work. It may cost you a few uncharged hours, but the benefits are realized in the real-world testing and learning that you receive, not to mention that extra level of innovation for the client's site.

If you're unsure of what you should invest your time in learning, spend some time on discussion forums or join networking groups like the ones we've discussed in previous chapters. Seek out freelancers in similar positions to yourself, and ask them what they are currently learning or researching—this is a great way to obtain a snapshot of what others are doing. However, remember that having unique skills puts you at an advantage; you don't want to be exactly like everyone else.

Go to conferences and join those industry groups we discussed in the last chapter—they're not only great for the social networking, but are also highly educational. And review your skill levels regularly; if you were to leave freelancing today and go back to an employment position, would you have the required skills and capabilities?

 What Skills Are in Demand?

A great way to find out what skills you should have is to look at local employment advertisements, and check out what employers are asking for. Some online job sites even carry statistics showing what skills are currently in demand.

Always remember that no matter how hard you try, you'll never be the expert on everything. Be selective about what skills best complement your existing abilities, and what you truly need to invest time in learning. Learning new skills doesn't need to be a chore; make these up-skilling tasks an enjoyable part of your routine, and challenge yourself to learn more every month. Have fun!

Case Study

Emily

It's been crunch time for Emily recently. The amount of work being offered to her by her fairly stable group of clients meant that she had to turn some of the work down, to avoid working every weekend.

With that in mind, Emily took a brave step and increased her hourly rate significantly. This has meant that some of her earlier clients have decided to shop around, yet Emily knows that in the longer term, this will be better for her. Having an increased hourly rate, plus having enough confidence to be more selective of the types of projects that she'll take on, means that Emily is set on a very good direction for her preferred lifestyle.

Of course, there will always be the infrequent weekend or late evening, but Emily is finding that her new rates and selectivity allows her more time to socialize and spend time on her own hobbies, instead of constantly worrying about work.

Emily also imagines that one day she might take on an employee, but there are no plans for that in the medium term. Emily doesn't want the overheads of an office or the responsibilities of employees right now. Life is good at the moment, and Emily is proud of her freelance achievements so far.

Jacob

Since we met him at the close of the last chapter, Jacob made the leap into leasing a small office not too far from his home. He was lucky that he managed to sign it up for a fixed twelve months, with an option for another year after that. This means that should he grow quickly, he can opt out of the lease after just one year. It certainly isn't the biggest office in the city, but it does have room for five desks and a meeting room, so he has plenty of room to grow over the next year or so.

He now has a part-time employee: a developer who works for him three days a week. Jacob has also made a few contacts with suitable and keen candidates, should he need additional staff quickly. The two of them are working out well as a team, although it has taken Jacob a while to grow accustomed to not only managing his own time and utilization, but also being in charge of making sure his employee has enough work and is bringing in enough revenue to cover his expenses.

Jacob has recently put signage on the office exterior, as well as overhauling his web site. This now portrays his business as more than just one freelancer, and he's keen to capitalize on this and grow the number of staff. Rather than just hire people straight away, however, Jacob plans to engage people as contractors for particular projects before offering them fixed-term contracts of three months, which he can use as a trial period. Jacob understands his strengths lie in dealing with people, so he doesn't anticipate needing to hire an account executive or salesperson for quite some time.

Given he has an office, and also a few contacts out there in the industry, he no longer has reservations about pitching for larger projects.

Jacob is excited about his journey so far, and looks forward to a rosy future with more staff and more billings.

Summary

We covered many topics in this chapter, because, after all, we're talking about the road ahead of you in your freelancing journey. We started with the idea of making big decisions about your future before discussing a few of the options you have available to you.

We looked at ways of keeping solo and increasing your profits by being selective with the work you take on. We dealt with retiring from freelancing, and the options of what to do with your client base if you do so.

We then looked at building your business from being solo to having your own team, whether you want to stay small but take on larger projects as well, or hope to grow your business as large as possible. We looked at the various pros and cons of outsourcing, and also considered coworking or virtual teams. We then discussed taking on employees. This is a big step for most people, and there are plenty of decisions to make and challenges to face. We also looked at what we need to do once we have employees—how to manage them effectively and keep a cohesive team.

We talked about how you can avoid losing touch with your skills, and the importance of keeping up-to-date with the latest happenings in our fast-moving industry. Finally, we caught up with our two case-study people, web developer Emily and designer Jacob, for the very last time—their gamble of entering freelance work appears to have paid off very well!

Good Luck!

This book may be drawing to a close, but your career as a freelancer or small business hasn't, so I'd like to wish you the best of luck in the future.

Just as you did when you first purchased this book, remember that life is a learning experience, and the web industry is an especially powerful example of this. Always crave to learn more: buy more books, read more blogs, articles, and magazines, ask others for advice, and take time to discuss issues and form opinions.

 Don't Throw This Book Away!

Refer back to this book when you need to, and remember that we all go through different stages; although you may feel that one chapter wasn't so pertinent now, it could be very relevant to you tomorrow.

Look for mentors from whom you can seek advice. Others have gone through every self-doubt and every decision you've experienced thus far, so learn from those who have walked before you. You'll be delighted to find that most people are very approachable and happy to give their advice and thoughts on a subject.

Question everything that you do regularly. Look for methods to improve the way you work, or ask yourself what your motivations are—you'll find better ways, new ideas, and lots of answers as a result.

Ours is still a relatively young industry, and we're sharing in a very exciting time in its development; we're all building the future through the work and the projects that we do today. Given that our individual visions of what the Web will look like in another decade's time are so diverse and rich in differences, it will be fascinating to see where it heads, and how we, as an industry, change along with it.

I look forward to seeing you there!

Index

THE PRINCIPLES OF
PROJECT
MANAGEMENT

BY MERI WILLIAMS

RUN PROJECTS ON TIME AND TO BUDGET USING THIS SIMPLE STEP-BY-STEP GUIDE

2ND EDITION

THE WEB DESIGN BUSINESS KIT

BY **BRENDON SINCLAIR**

DEVELOP AND GROW YOUR WEB DESIGN BUSINESS

THE WEB SITE REVENUE MAXIMIZER

BY **PETER T. DAVIS**
& **GEORGINA LAIDLAW**

UNLEASH YOUR WEB SITE'S PROFIT POTENTIAL